CONTENTS

[handwritten note: Marilyn, Many ou friendship give joy to many here at the lake Happy Painting fond regards ... Jan 29 2003]

Gilcombe Farm.

The days are shortening at Gilcombe Farm, the sweet smell of the orchards permeate the soft warm days of Autumn. The children delight in knocking down the ripe apples from heavily laden boughs. The Apples are tumbled into the Cider press to make 'Scrumpy' which is a rather intoxicating Cider.

On cold days years ago the Scrumpy was heated by plunging a poker heated in the open fire into the Tankard.

As Autumn passes we think of Christmas. The Robins little red breasts seem brighter than ever and he bobs around so busily on the cold Winter days we feel he would love to carry the Children's messages to Father Christmas.

Another year has passed at Gilcombe Farm and this is another book for you to share with us, we hope you enjoy it.

General Notes

Materials.

Brushes.

Instructions for each project list the specific brushes used. I find Natural hair brushes suit my style of painting best.

Note that brush sizes vary between manufacturers.

In this book I have used the following:

Raphael Martre Kolinsky 8404 round brushes,

Raphael Kolinsky Pur 16684 Liner brush,

Raphael Series 8254 Wash brushes (synthetic),

Raphael Series 8274 Fan brushes (synthetic).

I also use Yarka Kolinsky Sables which I highly recommend.

Paints.

I have used two brands of water soluble acrylic paint in this book, DecoArt Americana™ and JoSonja's® Artists colours. Conversion charts to other major brands can be obtained from your paint supplier or from Bobbie Pearcy's 'Color Match Source Book',

published by Bobbie's Tru-Color System™, 64 E. Marion, Danville, IN 46112. Tel. (317) 745-7535

Mediums.

The following JoSonja's® Mediums were used in conjunction with the Acrylic paints:

Clear Glaze Medium,

Flow Medium,

Retarder/Antiquing Medium (hereafter referred to as Retarder Medium).

Supplies.

220 grit Sandpaper (or thereabouts),

360 grit Sandpaper (or thereabouts),

DecoArt Decomagic Brush cleaner,

A quarter of a kitchen sponge wipe,

Frisket™ film (self- adhesive film which can be cut to shape to protect areas of your design while painting adjacent areas.

Flexi masking tape available at house paint decorator shops.

Preparation.

Preparing the Wood surface,

Sand in the direction of the grain then dust off with an old brush. Now Tack the surface.

Tacking

To Tack your piece means to clean away sanding dust more thoroughly than simply brushing. Commercial Tack cloths are available but these are impregnated with Oil based products and cannot be used with acrylic paints. I Tack with a slightly water moistened sponge wipe (about three inches square) which is compatible with the paint.

Base coat paint.

I use a Ramekin for mixing base coat colours. To keep it fresh ,cover with a damp paper towel. For overnight storage cover with plastic wrap. To store for longer periods old Film cassettes or baby food jars work well.

Setting up your wet palette.

I use a shallow rectangular plastic sandwich box. Line the inside with a thin kitchen sponge wipe (moistened with water and wrung out to prevent it being too moist). Over this I place a slightly damp double piece of paper towel, If you get this too wet, your paints will run into each other. Your wet palette is now ready for use. Always keep the lid on when not in use and your paint will stay fresh for several days.

Side Loaded Brush:

This technique is one of the most important strokes in Decorative Folk Art and can be achieved with either a round or a flat brush. **Try this method :-**

Using Clear Glaze Medium, moisten your brush and between Finger and Thumb ease out excess moisture from your brush, leaving a small quantity within the brush hairs. If you are using a round brush flatten out. Now using one side only of the brush, pick up a little colour and going over to your dry palette gently brush a ½" area, easing the colour through the brush hairs (the moisture carries the paint through the hairs). Intense colour should flow from one side of the brush fading as it approaches the other side.

Basecoating Design Areas.

Give any substantial area which needs a basecoat of colour a moistening of Retarder. You will soon discover just how much to apply, too little and your paint will not flow evenly, causing a
patchy appearance, too much and the area will not accept your paint, or will bead up.
   Pick up any puddles with paper towel then re-brush the area. Tilt your surface and (as the light catches) it should have a slightly textured look. Wait half a minute or so before painting.
Areas which have been moistened with Retarder Medium followed by painting must be dried completely (you can use the warm setting on a Hair dryer). After allowing your painting to cool to room temperature you can continue painting and building up colours. I find using a slightly moist Retarder base gives more flexibility in painting. Errors can easily be wiped away using a water moistened cotton swab. You will find liner work flows more readily on the "slightly moist" painted areas.

Floating Colour.
Colour can be floated on top of water or Retarder Medium to give a delicate or transparent effect and to facilitate blending.
Water. Moisten areas with water and use a wash brush (long Haired, flat brush) to add colours. I use water mainly when I am painting landscapes. I feel you get a softer look with a water base. It is necessary to work quickly as water has a fast drying time. When you are happy with your background, and before painting any more, you must dry with a warm setting on the Hair dryer.
Retarder Medium. Use as a basecoat in areas where you require longer working time to blend your colours or when you want to overlay a transparent colour on your already painted design..

Graduated Colour.
Have your selection of colours ready. Moisten the entire background area with Retarder Medium. Then, using a side loaded wash brush, begin painting at the top of the piece. Use a Fan brush to soften strokes. Next, rinse the wash brush and pick up another colour and paint across the area. Let the colours merge, softening them with a dry Fan brush. Continue until you are happy with the appearance. If the area starts to dry too quickly, soften what you have already done with the Fan brush and dry with a hair dryer, cool to room temperature the moisten with Retarder Medium and repeat the procedure.

Brush Blending.
Using the tip of your brush, pick up colour from your wet palette, deposit onto your dry palette. Now pick up another colour and mix it into the first. By mixing colours with this method you avoid cluttering up your wet palette.

Dry brushing.
Always put out fresh paint for this method of painting. You will find a round brush gives a more 'casual' appearance than does a flat brush.
   Keep your brush free from excess moisture and gently brush area's to give the desired effect.

COUNTRY
SLEIGH

Reverse design for
opposite side panel.

Gen © 1997 B1116.

Sleigh foot panel

4

COUNTRY GOOSE WREATH.

(Apple shown on the line drawing is separate)

Hole to pass twig through to support the Apple

Wood cutting line

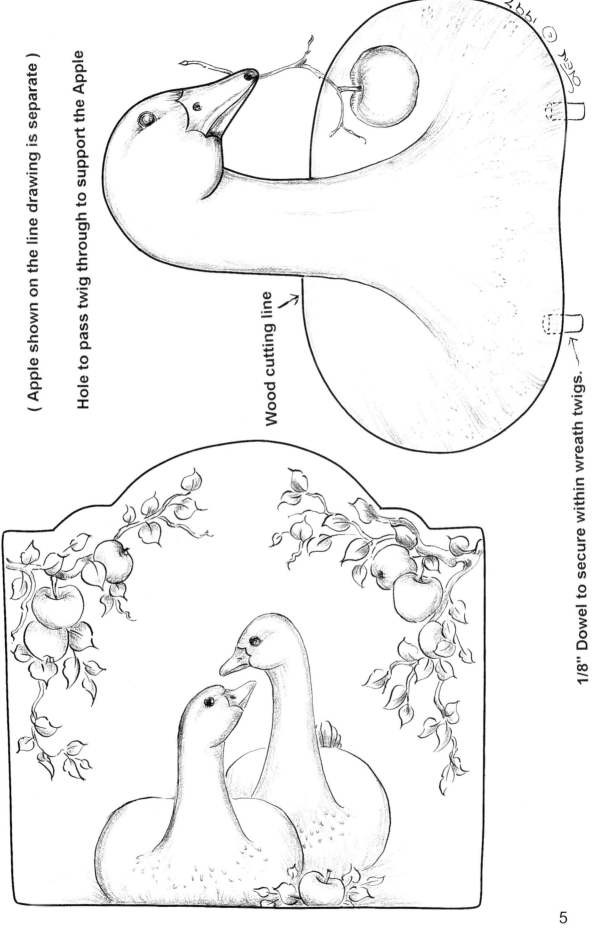

1/8" Dowel to secure within wreath twigs.

Sleigh head panel

5

COUNTRY SLEIGH

.Background colours.

| DecoArt | Buttermilk, |
| " | Williamsburg Blue. |

Antiquing and Painting colours.

DecoArt	Milk Chocolate,
"	Yellow Light,
"	Asphaltum,
"	Black Green,
"	Hauser Medium Green,
"	Deep Midnight Blue,
"	Raw Umber,
"	Raw Sienna,
"	Red Iron Oxide,
"	Moon Yellow,
"	Brandy Wine,
"	Georgia Clay,
"	White Wash,
"	Desert Turquoise,
"	Napa Red,
"	Eggshell,
"	Neutral Grey,
JoSonja	Warm White.

Additional supplies.

JoSonja	Clear Glaze Medium,
"	Flow Medium,
"	Retarder Medium.
"	Matt Varnish,

Frisk Film (low tack adhesive film).
Mix of Copydex + water 1 : 3.

Brushes.

#18 Flat Wash,
#2 or 3 Fine Liner,
1/8 Deerfoot,
#4 Fan,
#4 Round (natural hair),
#3 or 4 Old round (for Copydex mix),
Old Toothbrush,
Cotton Buds.

Background preparation

In 4 small containers prepare the following:
(a) Clear Glaze Medium alone.
(b) **Buttermilk** + Clear Glaze Medium 1 : ¼.
(c) Williamsburg Blue + Clear Glaze 1 : ¼.
(d) Stain mixed from **Asphaltum** +Clear Glaze Medium + Retarder 1 :4 : 2.

1. Using 220 grit sandpaper, sand the wooden Sleigh also the metal Runners if they appear slick to touch. Brush off sandings and tack with a slightly moist sponge cloth.
2. Basecoat the Sleigh interior with Clear Glaze Medium, dry and gently sand. Dust off.
3. Stain interior of Sleigh using stain (d), then dry.

4. Working one section of the Sleigh interior at a time, paint over the stained area with a coat of **Williamsburg Blue.** As this starts to dry, use a paper towel to pull back the moist colour exposing the stained background to give the pretty worn paint look. Continue with the rest of the interior. If you let the paint dry too much, use a moist Green scrubby to achieve the same effect. When you are happy, dry your piece.
5. Basecoat Sleigh sides and bottom with the **Buttermilk** mix, dry then lightly sand. Repeat with a second coat.

Note: Instructions for Metal runners are given at the end of the project.

Painting your Design.

1. Trace design and transfer to the Sleigh sides.
2. Using Frisk film, trace the outline of the groups of Geese, cut out and position on the Sleigh sides.
3. Using the old round brush (moistened with soap to protect the hairs) apply the Copydex mix as a Mask for the Apples on the design. You can dry the mask but only use the warm setting on the hair dryer.
4. Working on one side panel at a time, antique the background using your #18 Flat wash. Moisten area with Retarder and follow with brushing **Milk Chocolate** on the entire panel. Use your Fan brush to even strokes. If you have too much paint, gently wipe back with a squared paper towel, being careful not to disturb the masked areas. Dry with a hair dryer on warm setting.
5. Re-moisten panel with Retarder. Now with a brush blend of **Milk Chocolate + Asphaltum** add more colour to the lower edge of the side panels.
6. On a still moist area and using your Deerfoot brush, stipple **Hauser Med Green** behind the apple branches, softening as you work beyond the branch areas. Dry again (with warm setting on dryer). You can now remove the Copydex and Frisk film masking. If colour has seeped under the mask, use a water moistened cotton bud and clean interior design edges.

Geese.

1. Basecoat some Geese with **Eggshell** and some with **Buttermilk.**
Tip: When I basecoat large areas, I always tip my brush in Clear Glaze Medium before

picking up colour to give me a firmer background to work on, "try it".

2. For Geese in **Eggshell**, moisten with Retarder and shade with **Neutral Grey.**

3. On a still moist base, lighten areas with **White wash** then dry.

4. For Geese painted in **Buttermilk**, work as the Eggshell but shade with a brush blend of **Neutral Grey + White Wash. Lighten areas** with **White Wash.**

5. On a still moist base, using a brush blend of **Neutral Grey + White Wash,** form some feather strokes. These strokes are formed easier using a natural hair brush. Spread the hairs of the brush, it will naturally form a cupped shape. Now pick up a little **White Wash** and form feathery type strokes. Dry.

6. Working one group of Geese at a time, re-moisten with Retarder. Tint over some shaded areas with thinned **Desert Turquoise** to add interest. Do not overwork this step. Now dry.

7. Drybrush **Warm White** to highlight.

Beak.

1. Basecoat in **Georgia Clay.** Dry.

2. Using a sideloaded technique and a brush blend of **Asphaltum + Raw Sienna,** shade the Beak where it joins the Head, the Beak opening and the Nostril.

3. Using thinned **Hauser Med Green,** stipple the tip of the Beak to give a grass stained appearance.

4. Drybrush highlight areas with **Warm White.**

5. Linerwork the Beak opening with **Asphaltum.**

Eyes.

1. Form the Eye using your Liner brush and **Deep Midnight Blue.** Dry.

2. Using thinned **White Wash,** form a very thin 'C' stroke within the circle.

3. Linerwork the outer circle around the Eye with **Moon Yellow.**

4. Dot the eye with **Warm White** to give a glint.

Apples, Leaves and Branches.

Instructions for this section are to be found on pages 11 and 12.

Finishing your Sleigh.

Runners.

Mix **Deep Midnight Blue + Asphaltum**

2 : 1 with a few drops of <u>Matt</u> Varnish. Now basecoat Runners. Give two coats. Dry.

Antiquing Sleigh interior.

1. Moisten entire interior with Retarder, now darken corners with a mix of **Deep Midnight Blue + Asphaltum 2 : 1,** use your Fan brush to even strokes. Use a squared paper towel to

wipe back excess colour then Fan brush again Dry.

2. Protect the side design panels and Fleck the interior using an old toothbrush with a mix of **Deep Midnight Blue + Asphaltum 2 : 1** plus a little water. Dry.

3. On the side panels, protect the Geese with paper towel masks and using your old Toothbrush with a mix of **Milk Chocolate + Asphaltum 1 : 1** plus a little water, fleck the sides. Any areas you do not want flecked you can quickly clear with a water moistened cotton bud. Allow to dry for at least 24 hours before varnishing and another 24 hours or more before giving a wax and polish.

Tie-on Tag. Cut from ¼" Pine.
We put these on the Childrens Christmas presents, they then use them as tree decorations and are then hung on kitchen cabinet doors.

CHILDREN IN THE ORCHARD.
Background Colours
DecoArt	Williamsburg Blue,
"	Buttermilk,
"	Deep Midnight Blue,
"	Asphaltum.

Painting Colours.
DecoArt	White Wash,
"	Deep Midnight Blue,
"	Avocado,
"	Georgia Clay
"	Raw Umber,
"	Orchid,
"	Hauser Med Green,
"	Blue Mist,
"	Raw Sienna,
"	Yellow Light,
"	Red Iron Oxide,
"	Moon Yellow,
"	French Vanilla,
"	Desert Turquoise,
"	Neutral Grey,
"	Dioxazine Purple,
"	Flesh Tone,
"	Delane's Dark Flesh,
"	Delane's Cheek Colour,
"	Brandy Wine,
"	Napa Red,
"	Sapphire,
JoSonja	Warm White.

Additional Materials.
JoSonja	Retarder/Antiquing Medium,
"	Clear Glaze Medium,
"	Flow Medium,

Copydex + water 1 : 3,
220 and 360 grit Sandpaper,
Grey Transfer Paper.
The 11 ½" Plate is available from:
Stonebridge Collection,
   2 Mill St., Packenham,
   ON., Canada. KOA-2XO.
Or 4411 Bee Ridge Rd., Suite 256,
      Sarasoto, Fl., U.S.A. 34233.
Or in Europe from:
   Jen Sykes,
      Gilcombe Farm,
      Bruton, Somerset, BA100QE,
      England.

Brushes.
#18 Flat wash (3/4"),
#8 Natural Haired Filbert,
#4 Fan,
#3 and 4 Round ,
Old Round brush for using with
      Copydex mix,
#2 or 3 Liner,
1/8" Deerfoot.

Background preparation.

1. Sand your plate with 220 grit Sandpaper and brush off sandings.
2. Basecoat the plate back and edges with a mix of **Williamsburg Blue + Clear Glaze Medium 1 : ¼** , Dry then gently sand with 360 grit sandpaper. Now give a second coat then dry.
3. With a mix of **Buttermilk + Clear Glaze Medium 1 : ¼,** basecoat the front surface of the plate, now dry. Gently sand and give a second coat.
4. Moisten the Blue areas with Retarder then with a brush blend of **Deep Midnight Blue + Asphaltum,** antique these areas. Remove excess colour with a squared paper towel, even and soften strokes with your Fan brush. Dry.
5. Transfer the design, omitting the Leaves and Apples on the Tree.
6. Moisten the old round brush with soap then, using the Copydex mix, mask tree trunks, large branches, Geese, Children and Apples in the grass. Dry using the Warm setting on your Hair dryer.

Painting your Design.

Sky and Fields.

1. Moisten the Sky area with Retarder. Thin **Deep Midnight Blue** with Flow medium.
   Load the #18 Flat wash brush and starting at the top, work your way down towards the horizon. As you progress down the intensity of colour will decrease as the brush releases its paint. Ignore the hedge line at this time.
2. Moisten the two far away fields with Retarder then paint them with thinned **Hauser Med Green.** Now dry.
3. Re-moisten the two far away fields with Retarder then tint the horizon of the Right field with a brush blend of **Orchid + a touch of Deep Midnight Blue** and the horizon of the left field with a brush blend of **Deep Midnight Blue + a touch of Raw Umber.** Use your Fan brush to soften these colours.
4. Moisten the orchard field with Retarder then using thinned **Avocado,** paint in the Orchard field. Dry.
5. Re-moisten the Orchard field with Retarder. With a brush blend of **Avocado + a touch of Deep Midnight Blue,** shade under the Hedgerows. Shade under Children and Geese with a brush blend of **Deep Midnight Blue + Raw Umber.**

Fence and Hedgerows.

1. Outline the Fence using your Liner brush and a brush blend of **Raw Umber + Avocado.** Using the same colour but thinned, fill in between lines. Dry. Dry brush JoSonja **Warm White** to highlight.
2. Moisten far away hedges with Retarder then use your Deerfoot brush, stipple a soft haze hedgerow of **Blue Mist** and small areas of **Hauser Med Green** to give variation.
3. Moisten the closer hedgerows with Retarder and stipple them with **Avocado** using your Deerfoot. Dry.
4. Re-moisten the hedgerows and lighten some areas with **Yellow Light.** Shade with a brush blend of **Deep Midnight Blue + Avocado.** Very softly stipple **Red Iron Oxide** in some areas to add interest.
5. At the base and selected areas, linerwork clusters of twigs with **Raw Umber.** Dry.
6. Dry brush with JoSonja Warm White to highlight. Dry.

Trees.

1. Peel away the masked areas and transfer the tree apples and leaves clustering around the apples, other leaves can be freehanded in later.
2. Moisten the tree trunk and larger branches with Retarder then paint them with a brush blend of **Raw Umber + a touch of Avocado.** Dry.
3. Re-moisten these areas with Retarder and shade with a brush blend of **Deep Midnight Blue + Avocado** and for darker areas **Deep Midnight Blue + Raw Umber.** Dry.
4. Re-moisten again and lighten areas with thinned **Yellow Light.** Dry.
5. Dry brush the trunk and branches with JoSonja **Warm White.**
6. Linerwork the outline of the smaller branches with a brush blend of **Raw Umber + a touch of Avocado.** Thin the same colour and fill in the branches. Shade and lighten as in 2,3 and 4 above. Dry brush with JoSonja **Warm White** to highlight.

Apples.

Refer to the Apple worksheet and notes on pages 11 and 12.

Leaves.

1. Paint small one stroke leaves using thinned **Hauser Med Green,** make some lighter than others and also vary the colours by brush blending **Hauser Med Green + Raw Sienna.** Dry.

Continued on page 16

1.

2.

3.

4.

5.

6.

1.

2.

3.

4.

APPLE WORKSHEET.

Preparation colours.
DecoArt	Buttermilk,
"	Milk Chocolate,
"	Asphaltum.

Painting colours.
DecoArt	French Vanilla,
"	Moon Yellow,
"	Red Iron Oxide,
"	Brandy Wine,
"	Raw Umber
"	Napa Red,
"	Yellow Light,
"	Hauser Med Green,
"	Black Green,
"	Desert Turquoise,
"	Deep Midnight Blue,
JoSonja	Warm White.

Additional Materials.
JoSonja	Clear Glaze Medium,
"	Retarder/antique Medium,
"	Flow Medium.
Copydex.	

Brushes.
¾" or #18 Flat wash,
#4 Fan,
#3 or 4 Old round for Copydex,
#3 Round Natural hair,
1/8" Deerfoot,
#2 or 3 Liner brush.

Note: The following step numbers are the same as those on the colour worksheet on page 11.

Step 1.
Basecoat background with **Buttermilk + Clear Glaze Medium 1 : ¼.** Dry, then gently sand and repeat.

Transfer a minimum amount of design and then mask off the apple areas using a mix of Copydex + water 1:3 applied with your old round brush. Dry the Copydex mask using the <u>warm</u> setting of your Hair dryer.

Antique by moistening the entire background with Retarder then with a mix of **Milk Chocolate + Asphaltum 1 : ¼** antique the area, using a Fan brush to even out strokes. Dry on a warm setting.

Re-moisten the area with Retarder and using your Deerfoot with a thinned brush blend of **Hauser Med Green + Raw Umber**, gently stipple in a background that fades away into the Antiquing. Warm dry then peel off the Copydex mask.

Step 2.
Basecoat both Apples, tipping your brush first in Clear Glaze Medium followed by **Moon Yellow.** Dry.

Step 3.
Moisten the apples with Retarder then using your round brush and **Hauser Med Green**, paint in the Apple smile. Pat blend to soften. Continuing on the still moist base and using **Red Iron Oxide,** pull streaky strokes in the round form of the apple.

Note: If you should pull too much colour into the stalk and flower end of the apple, gently pull some out with a clean but slightly moist brush. Now dry.

Step 4.
Re-moisten apples with Retarder and shade the stalk area with a brush blend of **Hauser Med Green + Deep Midnight Blue**. Working on the still moist base, shade with **Brandy Wine.** Now dry.

Step 5
Re-moisten apples with Retarder, now shade dark corners using a brush blend of **Brandy Wine + Deep Midnight Blue.**

Step 6.
Still working on the moist area, tint with **Napa Red,** then using a brush blend of **Asphaltum + Deep Midnight Blue,** linerwork the flower end of the Apple. Dry then dry brush with JoSonja **Warm White** to highlight.

Leaves
Step 2.
Tipping your round brush with Clear Glaze Medium pick up **Hauser Med Green** and basecoat the leaves. Dry.

Step3.
Moisten leaves with Retarder and shade with **Black Green.**

Step 4.
Still working on the moist leaves lighten area's with **Yellow Light**, Pat blend to soften. Dry..

Step 5.
Re-moisten leaves with Retarder and tint edges as shown using **Desert Turquoise** in some areas, **Red Oxide** in others.

Step 6.
Using a linerbrush blend of the two greens, work in the stems Dry, then using **French Vanilla,** linerwork over veins and leaf edges to highlight. Dry. Now Dry brush **JoSonja Warm White** to highlight.

Branches.
Step 5
With a liner brush blend of **Raw Umber + Hauser Med Green + a touch of Deep Midnight Blue,** line the branches and stems. Thin the mix with Flow Medium and fill in the branches. Dry.

Step 6.
Using your liner brush, drybrush **JoSonja Warm White** to highlight the branch and apple stems.

Using your round brush and thinned **Hauser Med Green,** paint in the background leaves to soften your design. Vary the colours by adding either **Yellow Light** or **Deep Midnight Blue** to darken.

MINI LANDSCAPES.

Preparation Colour.
DecoArt   Buttermilk.

Painting Colours.
DecoArt   Jade Green,
"   Hauser Med Green,
"   Yellow Light,
"   Orchid,
"   Deep Midnight Blue,
"   Asphaltum,
"   Red Iron Oxide,
"   Charcoal,
JoSonja   Warm White.

Additional Materials.
JoSonja   Clear Glaze Medium,
"   Retarder/Antiquing Medium,
"   Flow Medium.

Brushes.
¾" or #18 Flat Wash,
#4 Fan,
#7 Round or Filbert,
#3 Round (natural hair),
1/8" Deerfoot,
2 or 3 Liner.

Background preparation.
Basecoat background with a mix of **Buttermilk +** JoSonja **Clear Glaze Medium 1 : ¼.** Dry then sand and repeat. Lightly transfer minimal design lines.
Note: The following step numbers are the same as those on the colour worksheet on page 11.

Sky
Step 1.
Moisten area with Retarder then using large round brush, lightly streak **Deep Midnight Blue,** working across the Sky from top down towards the horizon. Soften and even your strokes with the Fan brush.
Step 2.
Using your #3 round, pick up a drop of clean water and drop onto the Sky to make a cloud formation. Ease the water drop with the tip of your brush to enlarge or change the shape of the cloud. When you are happy, dry.
Step 4.
Moisten the cloud area's with Retarder then using your round brush and thinned **Charcoal Grey,** tint the lower side of the clouds. Clean your brush and stipple **Warm White** in the highlight areas. Dry.

Fields
Step 2.
Moisten all three fields with Retarder, now using your large round brush, wash in:
   Right rear field = Jade Green,
   Left rear field   = Hauser Med Green,
   Front field   = Brush blend of **Hauser Med**
                    Green+ touch of Asphaltum

Give the Front field a Grass tufted appearance by using your Fan brush and a short upward pushing stroke. Dry.

Step 4.
Re-moisten the fields with Retarder and tint additional colours for added interest.
   Right rear field.   Tint the horizon with a brush blend of **Jade Green + touch of Deep Midnight Blue.** The footpath toward the Trees with thinned **Asphaltum** and tiny touches of **Deep Midnight Blue.**
   Left rear field.   Tint a touch of **Deep Midnight Blue** under the trees for a hint of Bluebells. The horizon and the centre a brush blend of **Hauser Med Green + Deep Midnight Blue.**
   Front field.   Shade under the fence, hedge and footpath with a brush blend of **Hauser Med Green, Asphaltum +** a tiny touch of **Deep Midnight Blue.**

Trees and Hedges.
Step 3.
Moisten all foliage area's with Retarder. Use your Deerfoot to stipple in the various foliage colours.
   Far away Hedge. A brush blend of **Hauser Med Green +** a touch of **Orchid.**
   Trees. A brush blend of **Hauser Med Green +** a tiny touch of **Orchid.**
   Front Hedge.   A brush blend of **Hauser Med Green +** a touch of **Deep Midnight Blue** and at the base of the hedge the same blend but adding a touch of **Asphaltum.** Now dry.
Step 4.
Re-moisten all foliage with Retarder and add different touches of colour to give Form,
   Right Far Hedge.   In a small area **Hauser Med Green.**
   Trees. Brush blend of **Hauser Med Green + Deep Midnight Blue** to the shaded side (left) and **Yellow Light** to the lighter side (right).
   Front Hedge. Shade with a brush blend of **Hauser Med Green + Deep Midnight Blue** and lighter areas with **Yellow Light.** Dry then re-moisten trees and front hedge with Retarder. Tint the shaded area of the middle tree with a touch of **Red Iron Oxide** and the shaded area of the hedge with **Aqua.** Dry.
   Using your round brush and **Warm White, drybrush to highlight foliage.**

Fencing and Tree Trunks.
Step 3.
Brush blend thinned **Charcoal Grey + Hauser Med Green** and use your Liner brush to outline trunks and fencing as shown.
Step 4.
Using the same step 3 colour, thin and fill between the liner work. Dry then dry brush **Warm White** to highlight the fence.

13

Children in Orchard Continued from page 10.

2. Using a side loaded technique and a brush blend of **Deep Midnight Blue + Avocado,** shade just a few. Dry.
3. Moisten leaves with Retarder and Tint a few leaf edges with **Red Iron Oxide** and some with **Desert Turquoise.**

Geese.
Refer to the Geese section on page 6. For the three Geese in this design, use the **Buttermilk Goose** instructions .

Children.
Instructions for Children are given on page 21 with the following additions/changes.

Girls Dress.
1. Basecoat with thinned **Deep Midnight Blue.**
2. Shade with stronger **Deep Midnight Blue.**
3. Lighten with **White Wash.**
4. Tint some areas with **Dioxazine Purple** and others with **Desert Turquoise.**
5. Dry brush JoSonja **Warm White** to highlight.

Boys shirt, Girls Apron and Bonnet.
1. Basecoat with **Buttermilk.**
2. 1st shade colour- thinned **Raw Sienna.**
3. 2nd shade colour- Brush blend of **Deep Midnight Blue + Raw Umber** (thinned).
4. Tint with **Desert Turquoise.**

Boots.
1. Basecoat with **Raw Sienna.**
2. Shade with **Asphaltum.**
3. Deep shade with a brush blend of **Asphaltum + Dioxazine Purple.**
4. Linerwork Laces and Eyelets with a brush blend of **Asphaltum + Dioxazine Purple.**
5. Highlight with a dry brush of JoSonja **Warm White.**

Trousers.
1. Basecoat with thinned **Asphaltum.**
2. Shade and Linerwork with a brush blend of **Asphaltum + Dioxazine Purple.**
3. Highlight with a dry brush of JoSonja **Warm White.**

Face.
Refer to Page 24 for in-depth instructions.

Hands and Arms.
1. Basecoat with **Flesh tones.**
2. Moisten area's with Retarder and shade with **Delane's Dark Flesh,** Dry.
3. Re-moisten with Retarder, brush blend **Delane's Dark Flesh +tiny touch of Asphaltum** and shade further.
4. On a still moist base, lighten area's with **Warm White .** Dry.
5. Using thinned dark shade colour, linerwork Finger Nails. Dry.
6. Dry brush JoSonja **Warm White** to highlight.

Hat.
Refer to page 25 for in-depth instructions.

Grass.
1. Using your Fan brush and **Avocado,** pull brush upwards to form clumps of Grass.
2. Using your Liner brush and varying values of Green e.g. **Avocado + Raw Sienna or Asphaltum,** Add more strokes to the grassy clumps.
3. Highlight a few grass strands with **French Vanilla,** also some with **White Wash.** Dry.

24 hours later you can varnish with your favourite varnish and after yet another 24 hours your piece can be waxed and buffed with paste wax.

BASKET OF APPLES (Shelf Design)

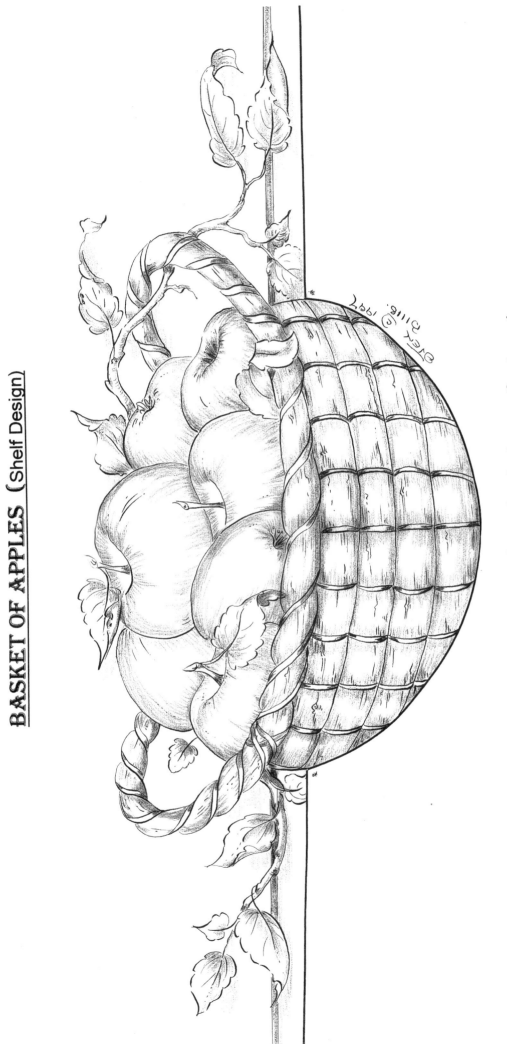

Sand to round the basket edge between the two *

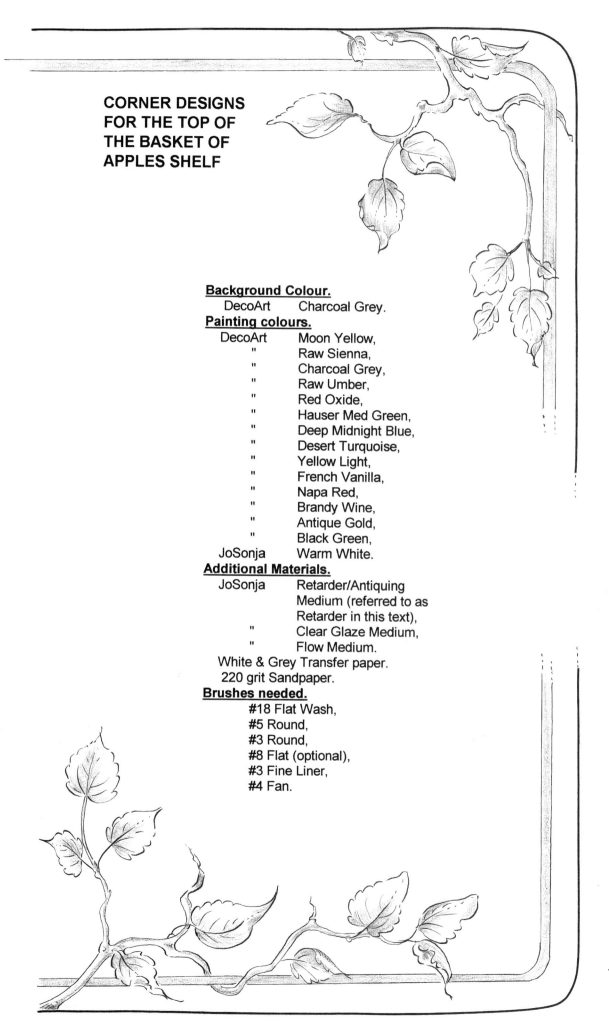

**CORNER DESIGNS
FOR THE TOP OF
THE BASKET OF
APPLES SHELF**

Background Colour.
    DecoArt   Charcoal Grey.
Painting colours.
    DecoArt   Moon Yellow,
        "   Raw Sienna,
        "   Charcoal Grey,
        "   Raw Umber,
        "   Red Oxide,
        "   Hauser Med Green,
        "   Deep Midnight Blue,
        "   Desert Turquoise,
        "   Yellow Light,
        "   French Vanilla,
        "   Napa Red,
        "   Brandy Wine,
        "   Antique Gold,
        "   Black Green,
    JoSonja   Warm White.
Additional Materials.
    JoSonja   Retarder/Antiquing
                   Medium (referred to as
                   Retarder in this text),
        "   Clear Glaze Medium,
        "   Flow Medium.
    White & Grey Transfer paper.
    220 grit Sandpaper.
Brushes needed.
        #18 Flat Wash,
        #5 Round,
        #3 Round,
        #8 Flat (optional),
        #3 Fine Liner,
        #4 Fan.

BASKET OF APPLES (SHELF).

Shelf preparation.
1. Sand your shelf with the 220 grit, working with the grain. Brush off sandings and Tack with a slightly moist sponge cloth.
2. Give the entire shelf one even coat of Clear Glaze Medium. After drying lightly sand and remove dust.
3. You are now ready to stain your Shelf. Into small container, mix **Charcoal Grey + Clear Glaze Medium + Retarder 1 : 3 : 2.** Mix well. Apply stain (working on one easily managed area at a time) with your #18 Flat wash brush, wiping back excess colour with a squared paper towel, then even out the strokes with your Fan brush. Dry then repeat until all is stained.
4. To antique corners, moisten the areas of concern with Retarder then, using a side loaded brush technique, darken corners and edges with **Charcoal Grey.**
5. Completely dry your piece before proceeding as you may lift the stain if it is not thoroughly dry.

Painting your Design.
1. Put Retarder, Clear Glaze Medium and Flow Medium into three separate small containers, also on your palette mix a small amount of **Moon Yellow + Clear Glaze Medium 4 : 1.** Now, using the white Transfer paper, transfer the boundary lines of the basket and apples.
2. Using your #5 Round brush and **Moon Yellow,** basecoat the area within the boundary lines. Dry and give a gentle sand with fine sandpaper (360 grit or finer). Now repeat this step.
3. Transfer the remaining design using Grey transfer paper, keeping your lines light and basic.
4. Moisten entire Basket and Handles with Retarder. Using **Raw Sienna** and your #5 Round brush with hairs opened out, pull colour across the Basket to give the appearance of Reeds. Work the Handles the same way. Dry.

5. Re-moisten entire basket with Retarder and using a side loaded technique with **Raw Umber**, separate the rows of Reeds and shade Handle.
6. Still working on the slightly moist surface of the basket, dry brush the reeds here and there to break up the flatness using your #3 round brush and a brush blend of **Raw Umber + Raw Sienna.**
7. Paint in the Laces on the basket and Handle with your #3 round brush and **Antique Gold.**
8. With a side loaded brush and **Raw Umber**, shade the sides of the laces and linerwork with same colour to clarify if necessary. Dry.
9. Re-moisten entire basket and handle with Retarder and Tint areas with a little thinned **Red Iron Oxide** and then other areas with **Yellow Light** and another (but smaller) area with **Hauser Med Green.** Evaluate your shading, if you need more depth at the upper corners shade with a brush blend of **Raw Umber + Deep Midnight Blue.** Pat blend to soften. Dry.
10. Using **JoSonja Warm White**, dry brush highlight areas. Dry.

Apples, Leaves and Branches.
Instructions are given on pages 11 - 12

Striping.
1. Using a smaller round or liner brush and **Red Iron Oxide.**
2. Shade areas with **Raw Umber.**
3. Lighten areas with a dry brush of **Antique Gold.**
4. Dry brush **Jo Sonja Warm White** to highlight areas.

Give your work 24 hours to dry before Varnishing. Matt varnish suits this type of design.
Wait another 24 hours before waxing and polishing.

APPLE GATHERERS.

1/8" dowel pin

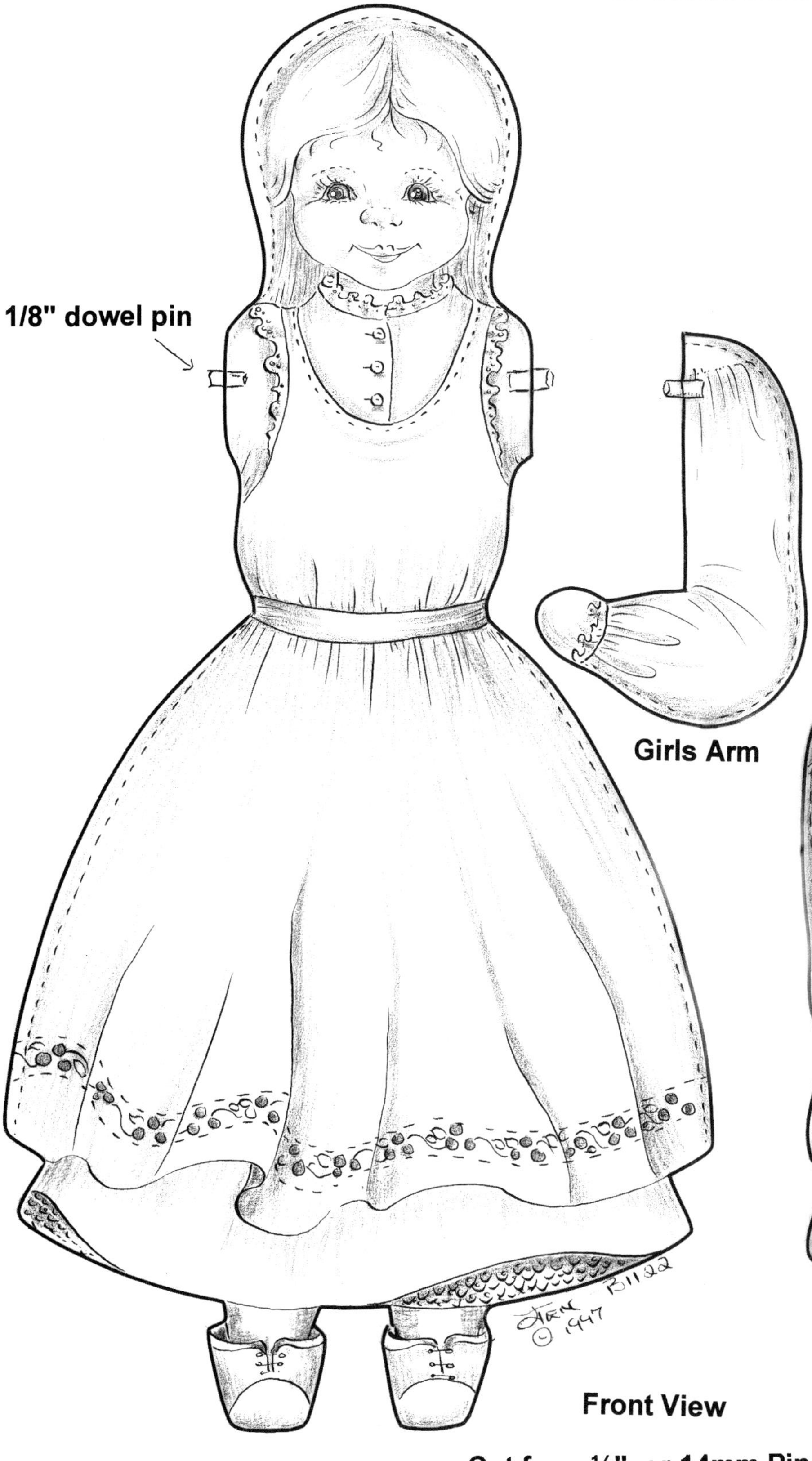

Girls Arm

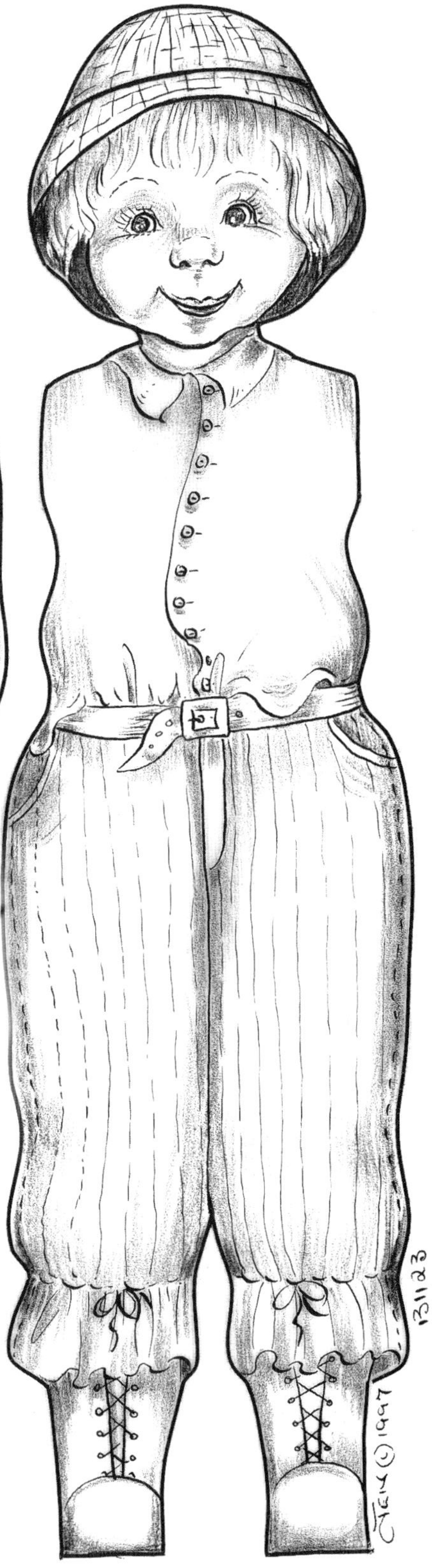

Front View

Cut from ½" or 14mm Pine

21

Back View

1/8" dowel pin

Reverse design for
opposite side Arms

Side view of shoe

22   **Sand to give a softer appearance using the dotted line as a guide**

APPLE GATHERERS (GIRL).

Background Colour.
DecoArt   Buttermilk

Design Colours.
DecoArt	Buttermilk,
"	White Wash,
"	Raw Sienna,
"	Hauser Med Green,
"	Moon Yellow,
"	Fresh Tone,
"	Delane's Dark Flesh,
"	Delane's Cheek colour,
"	Napthol Red,
"	Orchid,
"	Sapphire Blue,
"	Deep Midnight Blue,
"	Milk Chocolate,
"	Asphaltum,
"	Desert Turquoise,
"	Dioxazine Purple,
"	French Vanilla,
JoSonja	Warm White.

Brushes.
#5 Round (to base coat children),
3 Round,
6 Flat Wash (optional),
2 or 3 Liner,
8 hair Filbert (for applying Retarder).
Most of my brushes are made from natural hair.

Additional Materials.
JoSonja	Clear Glaze Medium,
"	Retarder Antiquing Medium,
"	Flow Medium,

Preparation.
1. Sand and Tack your Wooden blank.
2. Seal and basecoat whole figure with **Buttermilk** plus Clear Glaze medium 4 : 1. Dry and gently sand with 360 grit Sandpaper.
3. Repeat step 2.
4. Transfer the design.
5. Moisten dress areas with Retarder and (working one area at a time) basecoat dress and apron Lace area with thinned **Deep Midnight Blue**.
6. While the area is still wet and using a clean slightly moist brush, pull out colour in light areas of dress folds. If it looks streaky, wipe your brush and pat to soften lines. Now dry.
7. Re-moisten dress areas with Retarder and still using **Deep Midnight Blue** but not thinned, float in shaded area. Pat blend to soften. Now dry.
8. Re-moisten with Retarder and Tint areas with **Dioxazine Purple** also **Desert Turquoise**. Pat blend to soften. Now dry.
9. Dry brush highlight areas with JoSonja **Warm White**.

10. Linerwork Buttons with **White Wash,** the Thread is linerworked with **Deep Midnight Blue .**

Apron.
Note: The background for her Apron is the overall base colour **Buttermilk**, you can tidy the apron area if you like with another coat of **Buttermilk**. Now dry.
1. Moisten the apron with Retarder (working a comfortable area at a time). Shade folds with thinned **Raw Sienna** to give you a Cream appearance, dry.
2. At this point paint in the border design and stitches.
    Fruit- brush blend **Napthol Red** and **Raw Sienna** thinned with Flow Medium. Using your Liner brush, make irregular Berries, try to leave a light highlight area on the berry or come back later and dot with **Buttermilk** to highlight.
    Leaves are tiny one stroke leaves of thinned **Hauser Med Green**.
    Stitches are linerworked some with **Milk Chocolate** and some with a brush blend of **Deep Midnight Blue** and **Milk Chocolate**. Now dry.
3. Re-moisten with Retarder then using a brush blend of **Asphaltum** and **Deep Midnight Blue** (this will give you a warm shading grey), shade Folds and around the waistband. Pat blend to soften, then dry.
4. Re-moisten with Retarder and tint here and there with **Desert Turquoise** to add interest.
5. Linerwork gathers around waistline with a brush blend of **Asphaltum** and **Deep Midnight Blue**. *Note: Linerwork is easier worked on a slightly moist background.*
6. Drybrush highlight areas with JoSonja **Warm White**.

Lace.
1. Paint the Lace edges with a thinned **White Wash** to give a feel of transparency (leave neck and sleeve trims until you have painted the flesh areas). Dry.
2. With a side loaded brush, tip the lace edges to reinforce the **White Wash.**
3. Linerwork Lace holes and gathers with a brush blend of **Asphaltum** and **Deep Midnight Blue.**

Petticoat
1. Basecoat Petticoat areas with **White Wash** then dry.
2. Shade with a sideloaded brush blend of **Asphaltum** and **Deep Midnight Blue** then Linerwork Petticoat with same colour.

Stockings.

On the already basecoated stockings, shade with a brush blend of thinned **Asphaltum and Deep Midnight Blue**.

Boots.

Most Girls wore Boots in the Victorian era.

1. Basecoat with thinned **Raw Sienna** and then dry.
2. Shade in a sideloaded technique with a brush blend of **Raw Sienna** and **Asphaltum**.
3. Linerwork Eyelets and Laces with **Asphaltum**.

Face.

1. Basecoat Flesh and Hair areas with **Fleshtone**. *Note: Dip the tip of your brush into Clear Glaze Medium before picking up colour.* After drying give a second basecoat.
2. If you can still see your design lines, reinforce them with a soft pencil. If you can't then re-transfer them.
3. Moisten Flesh areas with Retarder and gently shade with **Delane's Dark Flesh**. Lighten Nose, Forehead, Cheekbones and tip of Chin with **White Wash**. Pat blend to soften. At this point work the eyes, return to the Cheeks later.

Eyes

Linerwork Eyes with **Sapphire**, Pupils linerwork with a smaller circle of **Deep Midnight Blue**. Add a comma of **Whitewash** in the corner of each eye and a dot in each pupil to give a sparkle.

Eye Lashes and Brows.

Linerwork with a brush blend **Asphaltum** and **Raw Sienna**. Highlight with **White Wash**.

Cheeks.

1. Moisten with Retarder, now using **Delane's Cheek colour** float in Cheeks, also the lower part of the nose tip. Pat blend to soften. Dry.
2. Re-moisten with Retarder and tint the sides of the Cheeks with **Orchid**. Dry.
3. Dry brush JoSonja **Warm White** to highlight Cheeks.

Lips.

1. Linerwork Lips with a brush blend of **Delane's Cheek colour** and **Napthol Red**.
2. Linerwork shading with **Milk Chocolate**.
3. Still using your Liner brush, dry brush JoSonja **Warm White** to highlight.

Hair.

1. Basecoat with **Moon Yellow**, pull your brush in the direction that the hair lies. Dry.
2. Moisten area with Retarder. Using **Raw Sienna** and your Round brush, "let the brush hairs open up to give you a hair like stroke". Vary the colour by adding a little **Asphaltum** to the **Raw Sienna**.
3. Shade Hair area behind the neck with a side loaded brush blend of **Asphaltum** with **Deep Midnight Blue**.

4. Linerwork hairs with a brush blend of **Asphaltum** with **Raw Sienna**, also some in **French Vanilla** and now a few in **White Wash** to lighten. Dry.
5. Dry brush JoSonja Warm White to highlight.

Ribbon.

Linerwork with **Napthol Red**, shade with a brush blend of **Napthol Red** and **Asphaltum**. Highlight with **White Wash**.

Apples

Refer to pages 11 - 12 for apple instructions. You will need a Glue Gun to fix apples in position. Varnish at least 24 hours later.

Boy.

Paints and materials as used for the girl.

Additional colours.

DecoArt **Midnight Green,**
" **Red Iron Oxide.**

Preparation.

Refer to Girl preparation.

Shirt.

Paint with colours and method as Girls dress.

Trousers.

1. Moisten a manageable area with Retarder, basecoat with a thinned Brown of **Raw Sienna** and **Asphaltum** 1 : 2, now, with a cleaned moist brush, wipe back area's which are lighter then wipe your brush and gently pat blend to soften. Dry. Continue other trouser areas.
2. Re-moisten with Retarder and shade using **Asphaltum** and in deeper shaded areas, a brush blend of **Asphaltum + Dioxazine Purple**. Dry.
3. Re-moisten Trousers and tint with **Red Iron Oxide**.
4. While areas are still slightly moist, Linerwork broken lines on the trousers in **Asphaltum**. Dry.
5. Our Boy has tied his trousers below the knees with 'Bag Tie', a common practice until the middle of this century. Bag Tie was normally used for tying sacks of grain or sheaves of Wheat. Bag Tie was also called Binder Twine, the Binder being the predecessor of the Combine Harvester.

   Linerwork the Twine with a brush blend of **Asphaltum + Dioxazine Purple**. Linerwork **White Wash** to highlight Ties.
6. Drybrush **JS Warm White** to highlight Trousers.

Boots.

1. Basecoat with thinned **Midnight Green**. Dry.
2. Moisten with Retarder and shade with a brush blend of **Deep Midnight Green + Dioxazine Purple**.
3. With the same shading colour, Linerwork eyelets and Laces. Dry.
4. Highlight Laces with a linerwork of **White Wash**. Dry.
5. Drybrush **JS Warm White** to highlight.

Face and Hands.
Refer to Girls Face but change eye colour to Brown.
Eyeball.
Using your liner brush with a brush blend of **Raw Sienna + Asphaltum,** circle the eyeball. Linerwork a brush blend of **Asphaltum + Deep Midnight Blue** and work the pupil.
Hair.
Refer to Girls.
Hat.
1. Basecoat with **Moon Yellow.** Dry.
2. With a brush blend of thinned **Raw Sienna +** a touch of **Asphaltum,** loosely colour the Hat. Dry.
3. Re-moisten with Retarder and shade with **Asphaltum.** Still working on the same moist base, tint with **Red Iron Oxide** to give additional warmth to the background colours.

4. Using thinned **Asphaltum,** linerwork weave. Dry.
5. Using **JS Warm White,** dry brush to highlight.
Belt.
The Belt is worked with the same build up of colour as the Boots.
Apples.
Directions for Apples are given on pages 11 - 12.

Leave your painting at least 24 hours before Varnishing and another 24 hours before Waxing and Polishing.

SWEET (CANDY) DISH

Background colours.
DecoArt	Buttermilk,
"	Williamsburg Blue,
"	Raw Umber,
"	Deep Midnight Blue,

Painting Colours.
DecoArt	Hauser Med Green,
"	Black Green,
"	Deep Midnight Blue,
"	Moon Yellow,
"	French Vanilla,
"	Raw Umber,
"	Asphaltum,
"	Red Iron Oxide,
"	Brandy Wine,
"	Napa Red,
"	Desert Turquoise,
"	Yellow Light,
"	Milk Chocolate,
JoSonja	Warm White.

Additional Materials.
JoSonja Retarder/Antiquing medium,
    "   Flow Medium,
    "   Clear Glaze Medium,
Grey Transfer Paper,
220 and 360 grit Sandpaper,
Copydex + Water mix 1 : 3
Candy Dish, available from :-
Valhalla Designs, 343 Twin pines drive,
  Glendale, Oregon, 97442, USA.
Or, Jen Sykes, Gilcombe Farm,
  Bruton, Somerset, BA 100 QE, England.
Brushes.
#18 Flat Wash or Sponge Brush,
#4 Fan,
#3 or 4 Round,
#2 or 3 Liner,
Old Toothbrush,
Old round Brush.

Dish Preparation.

1. Using 220 grit sand your piece then brush off sandings.
2. Using a mix of **Williamsburg Blue + Clear Glaze Medium 1 : ¼,** basecoat dish bottom, sides and handle. Dry.
   Gently sand and give these areas a second coat. Dry.
3. Using a mix of **Buttermilk + Clear Glaze Medium 1 : ¼,** basecoat the dish interior. After drying, gently sand and give a second coat. Dry.
4. Moisten the Dish bottom and sides with Retarder. With a mix of **Deep Midnight Blue + Raw Umber 1 : ¼,** antique the blue areas, wipe back areas which are too dark. Use your Fan brush to soften and even out the Antiquing. Dry. Now moisten the handle and repeat this procedure. Dry.
5. Transfer only basic outlines of the design, note the small pencilled leaves, these are much easier if freehanded in later.

Painting your design.

1. Using an old round brush and the Copydex mix, mask all the apples, the , using the warm setting on your
   Hair dryer,
   Dry.

2. Moisten the Dish interior with Retarder. Starting in the centre, antique with a brush blend of **Milk Chocolate + a touch of Asphaltum.** As you near the dish edges, change colour to a brush blend of **Hauser Med Green + a touch of Deep Midnight Blue.** Use your Fan brush to even and soften strokes. Dry using the warm setting on the dryer.
3. Remove the Copydex masked areas. Refer to pages 11 & 12 (Apple worksheet and notes) and complete your design.
4. Using your round brush and thinned **Hauser Med Green,** paint the shadow leaves pencilled on the design. Dry.
5. Mix **Milk Chocolate + a touch of Asphaltum** with water and using your old Toothbrush, fleck the design area. Soften the dots with a clean flat square of paper towel (a trick I learnt from my dear friend Helan Barrick) .
6. Stripe the Dish edge and Handle using your Liner brush and **Red Iron Oxide.**
7. Drybrush the stripe with JoSonja **Warm White.**
   After 24 hours varnish with your favourite varnish.

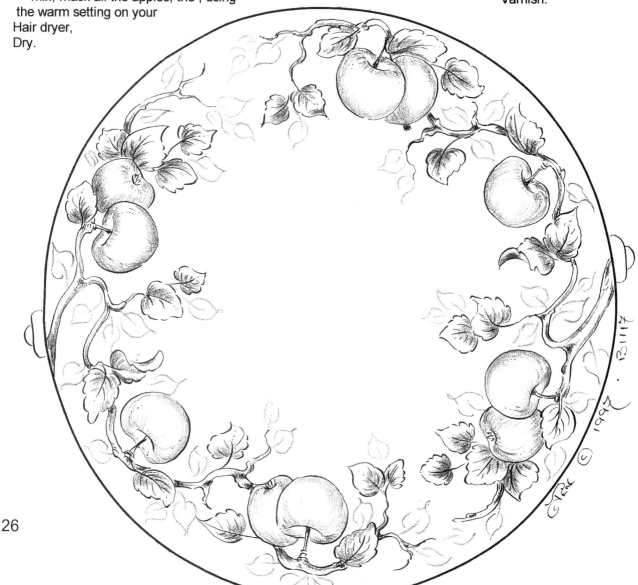

GOOSE AND GANDER CANDLE HOLDER.

Background colours.

DecoArt   Williamsburg Blue,
"   Buttermilk,
"   Deep Midnight Blue,
"   Asphaltum.

Painting Colours.

DecoArt   Milk Chocolate,
"   Asphaltum,
"   Black Green,
"   Hauser Med Green,
"   Deep Midnight Blue,
"   Buttermilk,
"   Eggshell,
"   Neutral Grey,
"   White Wash,
"   Desert Turquoise,
"   Raw Sienna,
"   Georgia Clay,
"   Golden Straw,
"   Moon Yellow,
"   Red Iron Oxide,
"   Brandy Wine,
"   Napa Red,
"   Yellow Light,
"   French Vanilla,
JoSonja   Warm White.

Tin Candle Holder

From Stonebridge collection,
2 Mill St.,
Pakenham, Ontario, Canada. KOA-2X0.
Or,
4411 Bee Ridge Rd., Suite 256,
Sarasota, Fl., U.S.A. 34233.

Additional materials.

JoSonja Retarder/Antiquing Medium,
"   Clear Glaze Medium,
"   Flow Medium,
Mix of Copydex and Water 1 : 3,
Matt Varnish,
220 and 360 grit sandpaper,
Grey Transfer paper.
Frisk Film, used to mask large area's.

Brushes.

#18 Flat Wash,
#4 Fan,
#3 and 4 Round,
#2 or 3 Liner,
an old Round brush.

Preparation.

1. Rough the bright Tinware with 220 Sandpaper.
2. Mix a few drops of Matt Varnish into **Williamsburg Blue.** Basecoat inside the Lampshade, candle holder area and handle. Dry then give a second coat and dry.
3. Mix a few drops of Matt Varnish into **Buttermilk** and basecoat the lampshade exterior and the band around the base. Dry then give a second coat and dry. Now pop it in an Oven at 150ºF (65ºC) for 30 minutes for a quick cure.
4. Moisten blue painted areas with Retarder and antique with a mix of **Deep Midnight Blue + Asphaltum 4 : 1,** now using a paper towel, wipe back excess colour. Finally, even and soften strokes with your Fan brush. Dry.
5. Transfer a minimal amount of design lines. Do not transfer the pencil drawn leaves shown on the design, free-hand them later.
6. Using your old round brush moistened with soap, pick up the Copydex mix and mask the apples and Geese. Dry using the warm setting on your Hair dryer. *Note : As the Geese shapes are larger, you can trace onto Frisk film and mask this way.*
7. With your large Flat wash brush, moisten shade with Retarder and Antique with **Milk Chocolate.** Use your Fan brush to even out strokes. Dry using the hair dryer on warm setting. Work the band around base the same way.
8. Re-moisten the shade with Retarder then using a brush blend of **Milk Chocolate + Asphaltum,** darken the lower quarter. On the still moist base, vary the colour under the apple design area with a brush blend of **Hauser Med Green + Deep Midnight Blue.** Soften where the colours merge. Dry using the warm setting on the dryer. Now remove the masking.

Painting your Design.

Instructions for painting Geese are given on page 6 and for Apples , branches and leaves on pages 11 and 12.
Colour plate can be found on page 38

Additional Instructions.

1. Moisten around the base of the Geese with Retarder and shade with a brush blend of **Asphaltum + Deep Midnight Blue.**
2. Using your Fan brush and a mix of **Asphaltum + Raw Sienna,** pull upward strokes to give the appearance of dried Grass.
3. Using your Liner brush and varying colours (**Asphaltum, Golden Straw, White Wash,**

Continued from previous page.

French Vanilla and a mix of Asphaltum + Raw Sienna), work in Grasses.

4. With your small Round brush loosely paint in shadow leaves, some with a thinned brush blend of **Hauser Med Green +Raw Sienna** and some with a brush blend of **Hauser Med Green + Deep Midnight Blue**.

5. Linerwork lettering with a Brush blend of **Deep Midnight Blue + Asphaltum.** Use a little Flow Medium in your colour to give you better Linerwork control. Dry.

6. With your Liner brush, dry brush JoSonja **Warm White** to highlight the letters.

7. Shade under the lettering with **Asphaltum** using the side loaded technique. Dry.
After at least 24 hours the whole project can be Varnished.

Handle area

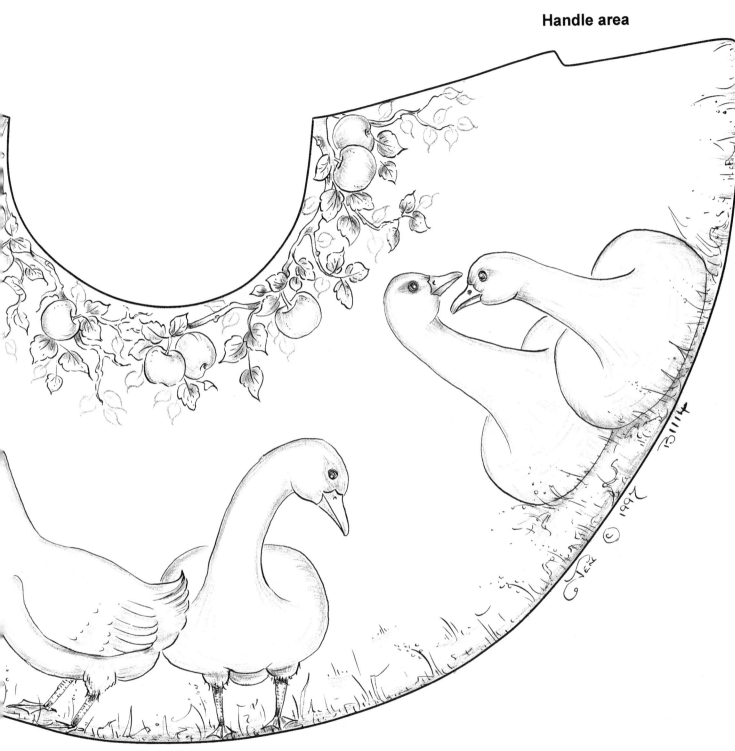

Transfer the lettering around the Candleholder base.

er where do they wander.

29

FARMYARD CHILDREN AND FRIENDS.

Table end section

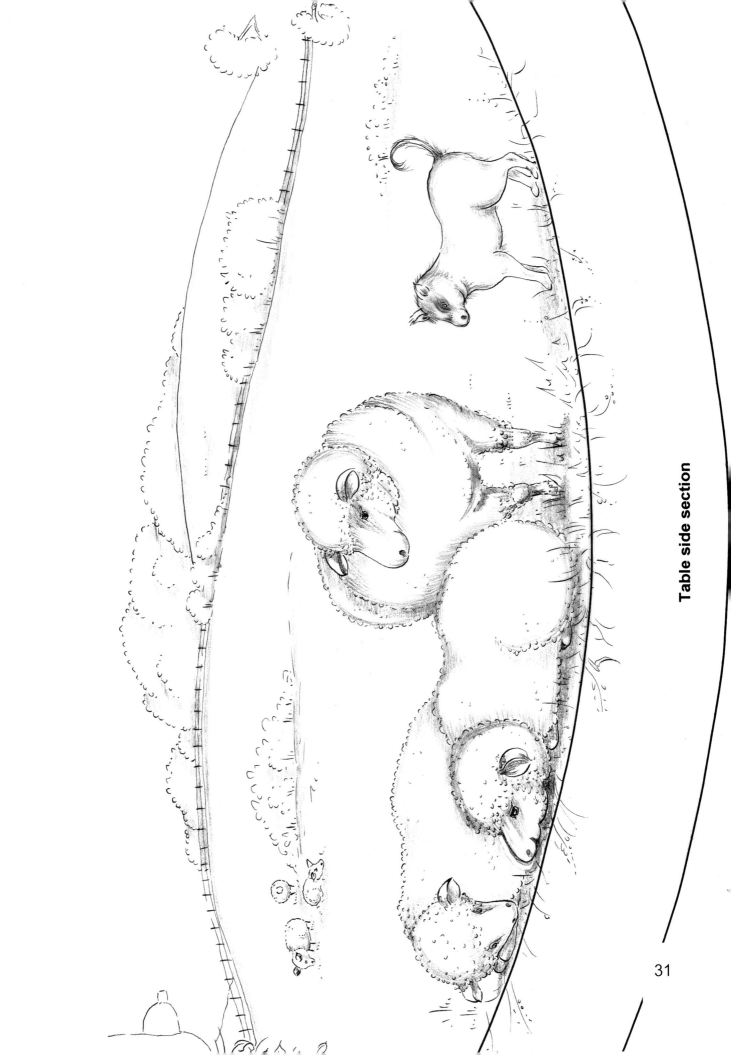

31

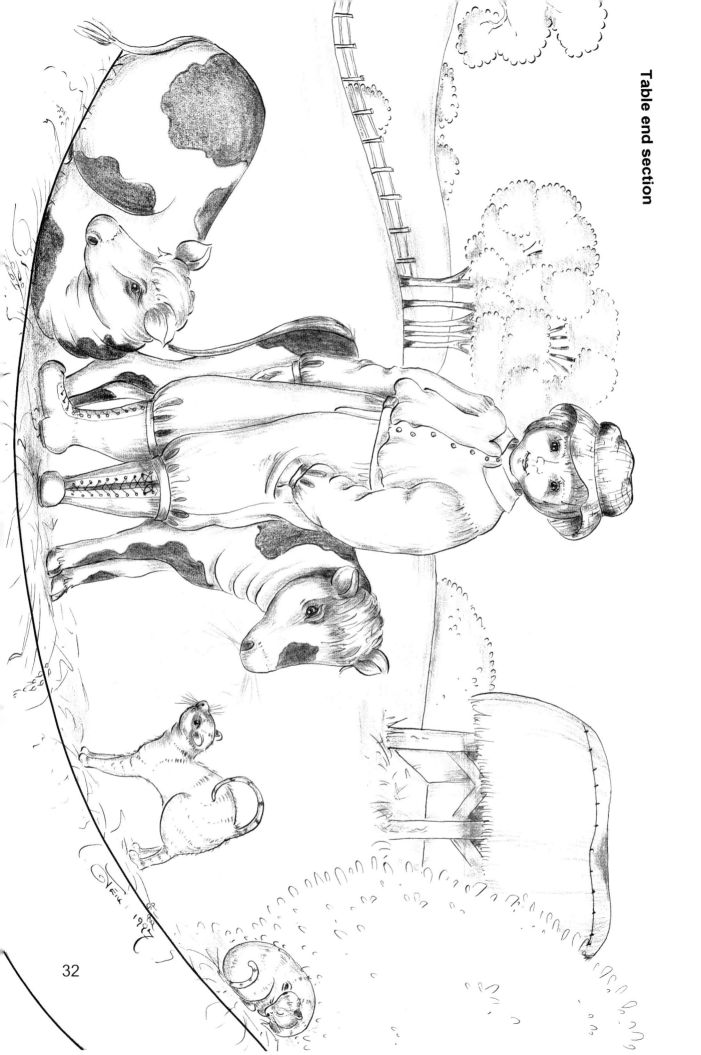

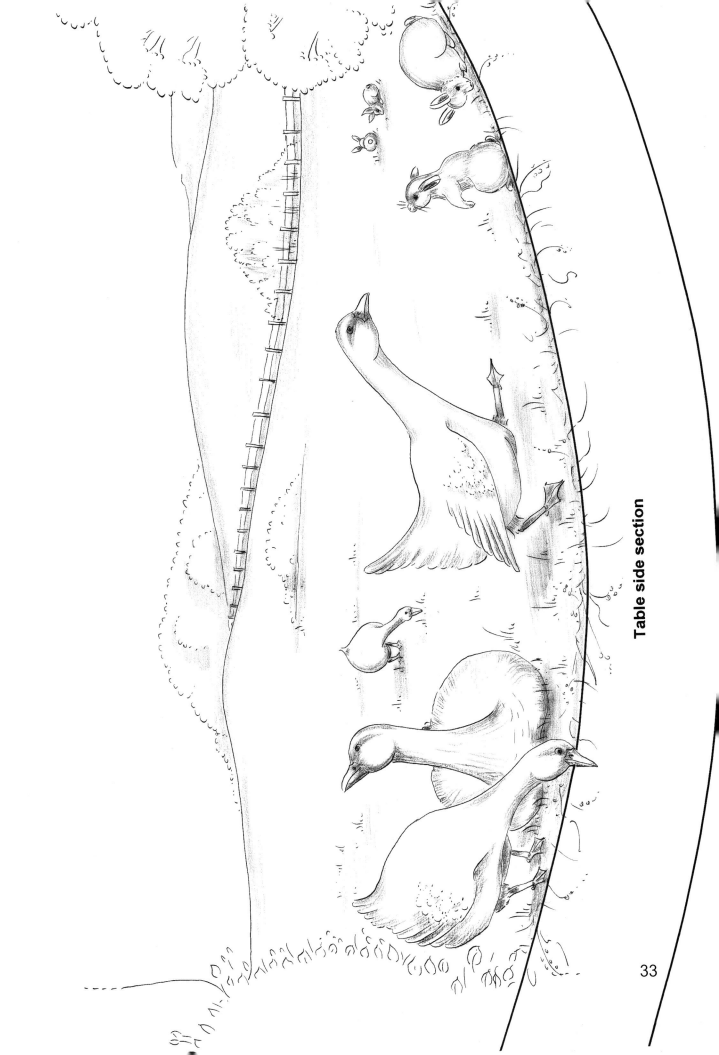

Table side section

FARMYARD CHILDREN AND FRIENDS.

Paint. Paints are JoSonja unless otherwise stated.

Background Colours.

DecoArt	Brandy Wine,
"	Buttermilk,
"	Asphaltum,
"	Black Plum.

Painting Colours.

Warm White ,	Smoked Pearl,
Raw Sienna,	Raw Umber,
Brown Earth,	Paynes Grey,
Yellow Oxide,	Turners Yellow,
Carbon Black,	Aqua,
Yellow Light,	Gold Oxide,
Cobalt Blue Hue,	Red Earth,
Sapphire,	Green Oxide,
Amythyst,	Storm Blue,
Brilliant Green,	Moss Green,
Jade,	Opal,
Burnt Sienna,	Teal Green,
Napthol Red Light.	

To be mixed,

Soft Brown = Brown Earth + Raw Umber +, Raw Sienna @ 1 : 1 : 1

Cream Mix = Smoked Pearl + Yellow Oxide @ 4 : 1.

Light Grey = Opal + touch of Green Oxide,

Dark Grey = Sapphire + Burnt Sienna @ 1 : 2.

And:

DecoArt	Flesh Tone,
"	Delanes Cheek colour.

Additional Materials.

JoSonja Clear Glaze Medium (referred to as Clear Glaze in this text),

JoSonja Retarder Antiquing Medium (referred to as Retarder in this text),

JoSonja Flow medium or your choice of brush moistener,

220 and 360 grit sandpaper,

Masking fluid (Copydex + Water 1 : 3),

Grey Transfer paper,

Slightly moist sponge wipe to tack your table after sanding,

Frisk Film (low tack adhesive film),

Flexi masking tape (masking tape that will work on a curve),

Brushes Needed.

1" Flat wash for base coating etc.,

#4 Fan used to even strokes and soften Colours,

#3 or 4 Old round, pre-moistened with soap to apply masking Fluid,

1/8" Deerfoot Stippler,

#4 Round, natural hair for general design painting,

#2 or 3 Liner, natural hair for Linerwork,

#6 Flat Wash. This brush is optional, you may prefer to sideload or float colour with a round or Filbert brush,

An old toothbrush for flecking the Red area's.

My Deerfoot is by Loew Cornell.

Background Preparation.

1. Sand your Table with 220 grit sandpaper then tack with a slightly moist sponge wipe.
2. Using a measure, mark a 1½" border around the table top edge then mask the outside edge of the design panel using Flexi Tape.
3. Using the oval side panel design as a Template, cut Frisk film ovals and position on the table side panels.
4. Using a mix of **Buttermilk** and Clear Glaze 4 : 1, basecoat the Table top panel. Dry, gently sand then repeat. Remove all Flexi Tape.
5. With a mix of **Brandy Wine** and Clear Glaze 4 : 1, basecoat the remainder of the table out side the design panels. Dry, sand gently then give a second coat. Remove Frisk film from side panels.
6. Using the **Buttermilk** mix as in step 4, basecoat the side panel ovals. Dry, sand and repeat.
7. Using the 220 grit sandpaper, sand away the paint on the Red area's to give an old distressed look. Tack away sandings.
8. Working on one area at a time through to completion, moisten the **Brandywine** area's with Retarder. Antique with a mix of **Asphaltum + Black Plum 4 : 1**. Use your Fan brush to even and soften strokes. Dry. Continue Antiquing another manageable area.
9. Protect the **Buttermilk** painted area's and using a mix of **Black Plum + Water,** fleck the Red area's of the Table with the old Toothbrush. Dry.
10. Trace and Transfer the designs to the table using Transfer paper.

   Note: The design is so large that I have broken it into four area's. In between these area's you will need to stipple in shrubs not completely shown on the design area's.

11. Using the old round brush and Copydex mix, mask children, bucket, animals, cottage, barn and the Tree trunks in the two groups of Trees at either end of the Table. When Copydex mask is dry, proceed.

Painting your design

Sky.

1. Moisten entire sky area with Retarder and follow with a transparent wash of **Cobalt Blue Hue.** Use your Fan brush to even out and soften strokes.
2. To make simple cloud formations using your round brush, drop a few drops of Water to make a puddle on the Blue sky. You will see the blue clear and give you an irregular cloud formation. This can be enlarged by pushing the water with your Round brush. When you feel happy with the clouds, dry.

3. Re-moisten the clouds and using your small Deerfoot and **Nimbus Grey**, stipple the lower sides.
4. Still working on a moist base, stipple **Warm White** to highlight. Dry.

Girl's Fields.
1. Moisten the entire area with Retarder.
2. Wash Left rear field with **Soft Brown** mix.
3. Wash Right rear field with thinned **Jade**.
4. Wash Front field with thinned **Green Oxide**.
   Dry gently with a <u>warm</u> setting on your hairdryer.
5. Re-moisten all three fields with Retarder and Tint the Right field with a brush blend of **Amythyst + a touch of Paynes Grey**, the Left field add more **Soft Brown mix** to shade. Tint front field with **Soft Brown mix** as it nears the Red border. Now a brush blend of **Green Oxide + Soft Brown mix** to give shadows to the left side of the cottage. Add more touches of colour to the fields to give added interest.

   Continue the three remaining field sections using the same procedure, not forgetting to moisten with Retarder before introducing the various colours. This will give you a lovely soft watercolour appearance.

Goose Fields.
Rear Right field :- Wash with **Jade**, tint with touches of **Amythyst** on the Horizon and thinned **Storm Blue** near the Fence.
Front Field :- Wash with **Green Oxide**, tint left horizon with thinned **Storm Blue**, the right upper corner with **Turners Yellow** and around the shrub and border edge with thinned **Soft Brown mix**.

Boy's Fields.
Rear Field :- Wash with **Soft Brown mix**, tint with **Raw Umber** to shade.
Front Field :- Wash with **Green Oxide**, applying more thickly in the distant parts of the field. **Raw Sienna** around the Barn, **Soft Brown mix** along the border edge.

Sheep Fields.
Rear Field :- **Turners Yellow**, tint with **Raw Sienna** and near to Fence **Soft Brown**. Using your Deerfoot, stipple touches of **Red Earth** to represent Poppies.
Front Field :- **Green Oxide**, tint with **Soft Brown** around shrubs and at the border. Making sure your area's are <u>completely dry,</u> remove Copydex mask from all areas. If by chance there are stray spots of paint, try to remove them with a Cotton bud, if unsuccessful, paint over them with the background colour **Buttermilk**.

Boy and Girl.
Head Face and Hands :-
1. Tip round brush in Clear Glaze Medium and basecoat all flesh and Hair areas with **Flesh Tone**. Dry and repeat if necessary.

Note: I suggest you leave Hands until after clothing is painted.
2. Moisten Face area with Retarder, now shade Hair line, Eye cavity and around Nose with thinned **Soft Brown Mix**. Pat blend to soften.
Note :- You may find it easier if you linerwork face details with thinned **Soft Brown mix** prior to shading.
3. Linerwork the girls eye with a brush blend of **Sapphire** + a touch of **Warm White** to form the eyeball. Linerwork the Boy's eye with **Soft Brown mix**. The pupil for both is an innerball of **Storm Blue**, a touch of **Smoked Pearl** each side of the eyeball and a dot of **Warm White** to give the eyes a twinkle.
4. Using your liner brush and thinned **Soft Brown Mix**, work in eyelashes and eyebrows. Highlight them by linerworking **Warm White**. Dry.
5. Re-moisten Face with Retarder then using **Delanes Cheek colour**, work in the cheeks. Pat blend to soften. Lighten cheekbones with a clean brush and **Warm White**.
6. Working on a still moist base, lighten Nose with a touch of **Warm White** and using **Delanes Cheek colour**, pink the tip of the nose. Dry.
7. Dry brush **Warm White** to highlight cheeks.
8. Re-moisten cheek area's with Retarder and tint the receding area's with thinned **Amythyst**.

Hair.
1. Basecoat hair using your round brush and **Cream mix**. Dry.
2. Moisten Hair with Retarder and shade with **Soft Brown mix**. Highlight lighter area's with **Warm White**.
3. Using your Liner brush and thinned **Soft Brown mix**, work Hair strands and follow with linerwork of **Warm White** to lighten. Dry.
Note :- after you have painted the girls bonnet and Dress you can linerwork the hair falling onto her clothing.

Dress.
1. Moisten entire Dress area with Retarder, now brush in thinned **Storm Blue**. With a clean Retarder moistened brush, pull out area's to lighten folds, constantly wiping your brush to clear excess paint. Pat blend to soften. Dry.
2. Re-moisten Dress with Retarder then strengthen shaded areas with **Storm Blue**. In area's of deep shading use a brush blend of **Storm Blue + Diox Purple**.
3. On a still moist base, lighten highlight area's with **Warm White**. Dry.
4. Dry brush **Warm White to give a final highlight.**
5. Re-moisten the Dress and tint over deep shaded area's with a thinned **Aqua**.

Apron and Bonnet.

1. Working on the original **Buttermilk** table top colour and working each article separately through to completion, moisten with Retarder then shade with **Raw Sienna**. Dry.
2. Re-moisten with Retarder and shade darker area's with **Soft Brown mix**. Dry.
3. Re-moisten with Retarder and shade under the arm and darker area's of the Bonnet with a brush blend of **Storm Blue + Raw Umber**.
4. On a still moist base, lighten area's with **Warm White**. Dry.
5. Drybrush **Warm White** to highlight.

Boots and shoes.

1. Basecoat with thinned **Soft Brown mix**. Dry.
2. Moisten with Retarder and shade with a brush blend of **Brown Earth + Raw Umber**.
3. Linerwork laces and eyelets with a brush blend of **Raw Umber + Storm Blue**. Dry.
4. Linerwork **Cream** to highlight laces.
5. Dry brush **Warm White** to highlight remainder of footwear.

Boy's Shirt.

1. Working on the original **Buttermilk** table top colour, moisten the shirt with Retarder and shade with a brush blend of **Storm Blue + a touch of Raw Umber.**
2. Linerwork details with the same blend then dry.
3. Dry brush with **Warm White** to highlight.
4. Re-moisten the entire shirt with Retarder and tint with **Aqua** in the shaded area's.

Trousers and Hat.

Work these two items separately through to completion.

1. Moisten with Retarder then using a brush blend of **Soft Brown mix + Raw Sienna**, lightly paint in a basecoat. With a clean Retarder moistened brush, pull out colour in lighter areas. Pat blend to soften. Dry.
2. Re-moisten with Retarder and shade with **Soft Brown mix**. Dry.
3. Re-moisten with Retarder and shade deeper shaded areas with a brush blend of **Raw Umber + Diox Purple.**
4. Linerwork details with a brush blend of **Storm Blue + Raw Umber**. Dry.
5. Dry brush **Warm White** to highlight.
6. Re-moisten with Retarder Trousers, Boots, Hat and girls shoes. Now tint shaded areas with **Napthol Red Light**. Dry.

Cockerel and Hen.

1. Basecoat all the feathered family with **Cream mix**. Dry.
2. Working the Cockerel and Hen separately through to completion, moisten with Retarder. Brush blend **Soft Brown mix + Burnt Sienna** and

loosely paint in feathery strokes, let the hairs of your brush split apart for this effect. Dry.

3. Re-moisten with Retarder and using a brush blend of **Soft Brown mix + Raw Umber**, shade the darker areas.

Comb and Wattle.

1. Basecoat these areas with thinned **Red Earth** then dry.
2. Moisten the Comb and Wattle with Retarder then shade the darker areas with a brush blend of **Red Earth + Brown Earth**. Dry.
3. Dry brush **Warm White** to highlight.

Eyes.

1. Linerwork dot of **Soft Brown mix**.
2. Linerwork pupil with a small dot of brush blended **Raw Umber + Storm Blue**.
3. Now a tiny dot of **Warm White** to give a twinkle.

Beak and Legs.

1. Linerwork **Smoked Pearl**.
2. Linerwork shaded details with thinned **Raw Umber**.

Tinting.

1. Re-moisten Hen and Cockerel with Retarder then, using **Napthol Red Light,** tint Comb, Wattle and shaded areas. With a clean brush and **Brilliant Green** tint the Cockerel's Wing and Tail feathers and finally in lighter areas touches of **Yellow Light**. Dry.

Chicks.

1. Moisten with Retarder then reinforce the basecoat using your Deerfoot and **Turners Yellow**. Dry.
2. Re-moisten with Retarder and using your Round brush, shade with a brush blend of **Gold Oxide + a touch of Raw Umber**. Dry.
3. Re-moisten with Retarder then with your Deerfoot and **Warm White,** stipple highlight areas. Dry.
4. Dry brush a little **warm White** to give you further highlight areas.

Legs.

1. Linerwork in thinned **Gold Oxide**.
2. Shade with thinned **Raw Umber**.
3. Linerwork **Warm White** to highlight.

The eyes and Beaks are painted as their parents.

Sheep.

Paint Sheep one at a time as follows:

1. Using your Table top colour **Buttermilk** as the base, moisten the Sheep with Retarder.
2. With your Round brush shade areas with **Raw Sienna**. Dry.
3. Re-moisten with Retarder and shade darker areas with a brush blend of **Soft Brown mix + Raw Umber**.
4. On the still moist base stipple Warm White (not the face area) being careful not to encroach into dark shaded areas at this time. Dry.

Continued on page 40.

5. Stipple **Warm White** again on the dry background to reinforce the woolly texture drifting slightly onto the shaded areas.

Ears.
1. Tint the inside of the Ear with a thinned brush blend of **Red Earth + Soft Brown mix.**
2. Shade with **Raw Umber.**

Eyes.
1. Linerwork a **Raw Sienna** dot. Dry.
2. Linerwork the pupil with a brush blend of **Raw Umber + Soft Brown mix.**
3. Dot with **Warm White** for a glint in the Eye.
4. Linerwork **Warm White** to form eyelids and eye lashes.
5. Linerwork **Soft Brown mix** to separate eyelashes and deepen colour around the eye.

Nose.
1. Work a 'C' stroke in **Raw Umber** to form the nostril area.
2. Using **Warm White**, linerwork the part of the 'C' stroke to highlight.

All Sheep.
When all Sheep are painted, moisten them with Retarder and tint receding areas with thinned **Amythyst**. Dry.
The Hooves disappear into the grass and so do not need painting.

Geese.
1. Basecoat all Geese with **Light Grey mix.** Dry.
2. Working on one goose at a time, moisten with Retarder and shade with **Dark Grey mix**.
3. On a still moist base, lighten areas with **Warm White**. Dry.
4. Re-moisten with Retarder then using a side-loaded technique with **Dark Grey mix**, separate the Wing feathers.
5. With the same paint, 'feather' stroke the feathers at the base of the neck, the small wing feathers and the Tail feathers.
6. Using your round brush loaded with fresh **Warm White,** spread the brush to separate the hairs and gently touch the already painted feathering of steps 4 and 5 to highlight. Dry.
7. Dry brush **Warm White** to highlight the very lightest area's.

Eye.
1. Linerwork a solid circle of **Storm Blue**. Dry.
2. Use **Warm White** and give the circle a 'C' stroke.
3. Outline the Eye with **Yellow Oxide**.
4. Outline the yellow liner circle with a brush blend of **Light and Dark Grey mixes.**
5. Add a dot of **Warm White** for a glint in the Eye.

Beak, Legs and Feet.
1. Linerwork with **Gold Oxide**. Dry.
2. Shade and linerwork with **Raw Umber**.
3. Highlight with a linerbrush of **Warm White.**

Calves.
1. The basecoat for the Calves is the original **Buttermilk** tabletop colour.
   Moisten a calf with Retarder then using a brush blend of **Soft Brown mix + a touch of Raw Umber**, shade the overall shape of the calf, also the folds in the coat, the eye cavity which softly finishes above the Nostrils, around and inside the Ear and where one Leg shades another. Dry.
2. Re-moisten the Calf with Retarder then with a thinned brush blend of **Red Earth + Soft Brown mix,** paint in the Nose and inside the Ears.
3. Still on a moist base, with a brush blend of **Raw Umber + a touch of Carbon Black** and a round brush, paint in the dark pigmented areas of the Calf. Now using the same colour and your Liner brush, liner the Hairs where they overlap lighter areas and the longer curly hairs between the Ears. Dry.
4. Re-moisten the Calf in areas you feel need further shading, including the inside of the ears and reinforce with the step 1 shade colour.

Eyes.
1. Linerwork the Eye with a brush blend of **Raw Umber + Storm Blue.** Dry.
2. With **Warm White** give the eye a tiny 'C' stroke and add a tiny dot for a glint, then linerwork the eye lashes.
3. Linerwork a brush blend of **Soft Brown mix + Raw Umber** to give more detail around the Eye and to separate the light Eyelashes.

Nostril and Mouth.
1. With a brush blend of **Raw Umber + Storm Blue**, give the Nostril a 'C' stroke.
2. With a sideloaded brush of **Warm White**, highlight the upper side of the Nostril.
3. Linerwork the mouth using the Nostril colour.

Finalizing the Calf.
As with the sheep, the hooves disappear into the grass. Use **Warm White** and dry brush highlight areas.

Cats.
1. Moisten the entire Cat with Retarder and give him a thinned basecoat of **Raw Sienna**. Dry.
2. Re-moisten with Retarder and shade with the **Soft Brown mix.**
3. Using your Liner brush and the **Soft Brown mix**, work the rows of striped hairs and his outline to fluff him up a little, also dot his eye and work his whiskers.
4. Pink the inside of the ears with thinned **Red Earth** plus a touch of **Soft Brown mix**. Dry.
5. Shade the pink of the ear with a touch of **Soft Brown mix.**
6. Using **Warm White**, linerwork hairs to soften and dot the eye to give a sparkle.
7. Dry brush **Warm White** to highlight areas.

8. Moisten the entire Cat with Retarder and Tint the shaded upper neck area and around the Tail with a touch of **Napthol Red Light.**

Rabbits.

1. Basecoat with **Cream mix.** Dry.
2. Moisten with Retarder, now lightly brush the Rabbits with **Soft Brown mix**, heavier in the more shaded area's. Pat blend to soften. Dry.
3. Re-moisten with Retarder then using a brush blend of **Soft Brown mix + Brown Earth**, shade the darker areas.
4. Using the same shading colour, linerwork the Eyes, Whiskers and Fur. Dry.
5. Using **Warm White** paint the Tails. Dry.
6. Shade the base of the Tail with **Raw Sienna.**
7. Drybrush **Warm White** to highlight the lighter body area's.
8. Re-moisten the Rabbits with Retarder and Tint shade area's with **Red Earth.**

Shrubs, Trees, Hedgerows and Fencing.

Work on one item at a time through to completion before going on to the next.
1. To give the Foliage a softer appearance, moisten with Retarder and proceed as follows.
2. Using your Deerfoot brush, stipple various colours:
a) Far away Hedges, thinned brush blend of **Green Oxide + Paynes Grey.** Dry. Re-moisten with Retarder and stipple on **Green Oxide.** Tint with a touch of **Amythyst.**
b) Vary the remaining Hedgerows , shrubs and Trees with **Jade, Green Oxide** and a mix of **Moss Green + Raw Umber.** Dry. Re-moisten with Retarder and shade with a brush blend of **Raw Umber + Paynes Grey** or **Raw Umber + Teal Green.** Dry. Re-moisten with Retarder and Tint in various area's with any of these suggested colours: **Brown Earth, Red Earth, Brilliant Green** or **Aqua.**

Leaves.(2 shrubs).

Using your round brush and varying your greens, paint tiny one stroke leaves.

Tree Trunks, branches and Fencing.

Using your liner brush with a brush blend of **Green Oxide + Raw Umber**, paint in these items.

Cottage.

1. Using the buttermilk table top as the background, moisten the entire cottage and Thatch with Retarder, paint **Soft Brown mix** on Thatch and Tint the walls with a thinned brush blend of **Red Earth + Raw Sienna.**
2. Working on a still moist base, paint in the following:-
Chimney and Door = **Red Earth.**
Window panes = **Dark Grey mix.**
Door and Window frames = **Soft Brown mix.**
Dry.

3. Re-moisten entire cottage with Retarder then using a brush blend of **Soft Brown mix + Raw Umber**, shade the Thatch.
4. Working on a still moist base, shade the cottage walls under the Thatch with a brush blend of thinned **Raw Umber + Paynes Grey.**
5. With your Deerfoot and **Avocado**, stipple the climbing Roses.
6. Linerwork Beams with a brush blend of **Soft Brown mix + Raw Umber**, and the window frame with a brush blend of **Raw Umber + Paynes Grey.**
7. Roses are a brush blend of **Red Earth + Warm White.**
8. Highlight window panes with a dry brush of **Warm White.**

Barn.

1. Moisten entire Barn with Retarder and paint the Thatch as you did for the Cottage.
2. The interior walls shade with **Soft Brown mix.** In darker area's shade with a brush blend of **Soft Brown mix + Storm Blue.**
3. The beams are lightly painted with a brush blend of **Soft Brown mix + a touch of Avocado.**
4. With **Soft Brown mix**, linerwork Beams and stipple the Barn floor.

Bucket.

1. Basecoat with **Light Grey mix.** Dry.
2. Moisten with Retarder then with **Dark Grey mix**, shade and linerwork to define area's. Dry.
3.Re-moisten with Retarder. Tint **Aqua** on the receding left side and **Raw Sienna** on the right side. Dry.
4. Dry brush **Warm White** to highlight.
5. Using your round brush, stipple Grain in the Bucket with a brush blend of **Raw Sienna + Soft Brown mix**, add a little **Raw Umber** to the blend to stipple the shaded area's.

Completing your design.

With various colours, namely **Raw Sienna, Soft Brown mix,** and **Soft Brown mix + more Raw Umber** with Highlighting in **Cream mix,**
linerwork dried Hay around the base of the design spilling over onto the border.

After 24 hours give your piece a seal with JoSonja Clear Glaze Medium and dry.

Varnish with your choice of water based Varnish. I used Polyvine Satin + Polyvine Dead flat 1 : 1. Give the Table top 4 coats and the remainder 2 coats.

After at least another 48 hours gently wax with paste wax applying with an old green scrubby and buffing with a soft cloth.

Side panel designs can be found on page 52.

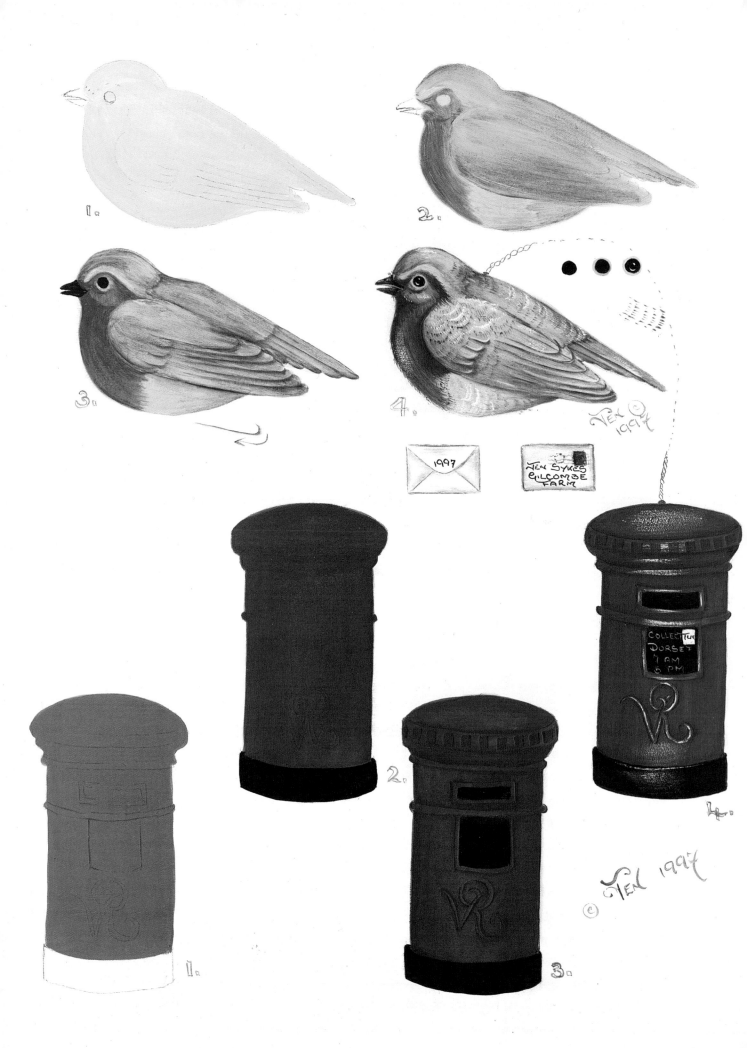

ROBINS AND POST BOX

Painting Colours.

DecoArt	Moon Yellow,
"	Country Red,
"	Black Plum,
"	Driftwood,
"	French Vanilla,
"	Raw Sienna,
"	Asphaltum,
"	Deep Midnight Blue,
"	Lamp Black,
"	Desert Turquoise,
"	Cadmium Orange,
"	Cadmium Yellow,
JoSonja	Warm White.

Additional Materials

JoSonja	Clear Glaze Medium,
"	Retarder/Antiquing Medium,
"	Flow Medium or your choice of brush moistener.

Brushes.

#6 or 8 Mongoose Filbert to apply Retarder,
#4 Round (natural hair) for general painting.
#2 or 3 Liner,
#6 Flat wash.

Procedure

Robin.

1. Basecoat with **Moon Yellow + Clear Glaze Medium at 1 : ¼**. Dry. Now transfer your design guide lines.
2. Moisten entire Robin with Retarder, wait 30 seconds and proceed. With a brush blend of **Cad Orange + Cad Yellow,** paint his Breast. Tummy and Eyebrow paint **Driftwood**. The remainder paint with a thinned mix of **Asphaltum + Raw Sienna at 2 : 1.** Dry.
3. Using your Flat brush dressed with Clear Glaze Medium, side load with **Asphaltum** and shade under all feathers. Using the same method shade other area's as shown. To give more depth of colour in darker shaded area's add a touch of **Deep Midnight Blue** to the above colour. Moisten the Robins breast with Retarder and using your round brush paint it in **Country Red.** Pat blend to soften. Dry.
4. Moisten entire Robin with Retarder. Shade the Breast with a brush blend of **Country Red + Deep Midnight Blue.**
   Using your round brush, blend **Asphaltum + Raw Sienna.** Slightly press open the hairs of the

brush and gently touch the painting surface to give you a feathery type stroke as shown. Dry.
   Now, using the same procedure, pick up **French Vanilla** and highlight the feathers.
Linerwork **French Vanilla** on the light edge of the Feathers. Using **Cad Yellow,** circle the eye and put in a **Warm White** dot for a twinkle. Linerwork the Beak with **Warm White** then dry brush **Warm White** to highlight. Dry.
   Moisten the underside of his Tummy and Tail feathers with Retarder and tint with **Aqua.**

Post Box

1. Basecoat with a mix of **Cad Orange + Cad Yellow + Clear Glaze Medium at 1 ; 1 ; ¼.** Dry. Sand lightly and repeat. Transfer your design.
2. Moisten the entire Box with Retarder and wash in **Country Red,** keeping the outer edges darker. Solidly paint the base **Lamp Black.** Dry.
3. Using your flat brush dressed with Clear Glaze Medium, pick up a side load of a mix of **Black Plum + Country Red at 1 ; 1** and shade the sides and box mouldings. **VR** means the box was made in the reign of Queen Victoria.
   Fill in the letter hole and collection plate using **Lamp Black.**
4. Linerwork lettering **Warm White** and the Day plate in **Lamp Black.** Dry brush **Warm White** to highlight the mouldings and lighter area's of the box. Dry.
5. After 24 hours Varnish with your favourite Varnish, remembering that Post Boxes are normally fairly shiny.

A reference book entitled 'Old Letter Boxes' by Martin Robinson can be obtained by mail from :
   Shire Publications Ltd.,
      Cromwell House, Church Street,
      Princes Risborough, Buckinghamshire,
      HP279AJ, England.
   Price £ 2.25
Or can be purchased on a visit to :
   Bath Postal Museum, 8 Broad Street,
                        Bath, BA15LJ

   Bruce Castle Museum, Lordship Lane,
                        London, N178NU.

   National Postal Museum, King Edwards Building
                        King Edwards Street,
                        London EC1A 1LP

CHRISTMAS MESSAGES
SLEIGH DESIGN

44

A

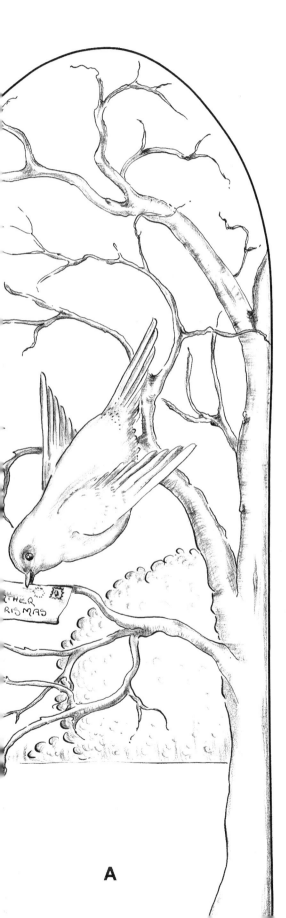

A

COFFEE BREAK TITBITS

The English Robin is the National Bird of England. 'Robin redbreast' is a fairly small songbird, probably our best songster especially in the spring when it often perches in the tops of trees and sings without repeating itself.

Our Robin is a completely different bird from the American model being almost half the size of its American namesake.

As well as being a good singer it is also a very territorial bird and will defend it's garden against all intruders but at the same time can become very tame, even entering your house and perching on tables.

The English Robin usually makes a cosy little nest in a bank but also often builds in Garden sheds. Under patio roofs and on several occasions on Farm machinery at Gilcombe.

Robins feature on more English Christmas cards than just about any other birds or animals and the festive season just wouldn't be the same without them.

Post boxes are sometimes called Letter boxes, Pillar boxes or Mail boxes have been around for over 150 years.

They can be round octagonal, Hexagonal or fitted flush into a wall or the side of a house or Post office.

The oldest one still in use in England is near Sherborne in Dorset and was made in 1853, but older one's do exist in museums, addresses of which are included in one of the projects in this book.

The British Post box is always painted Red and carries the cipher of the King or Queen reigning at the time the box was made. VR is Victorian, the VR standing for Victoria Regina. E R is Edward Rex and also Elizabeth Regina, GR is George Rex

A

Match A's and B's to assemble
the design for the Sleigh top

46

B

A

B

B

B

Transfer all Ivy in the later stages
of painting the design.

47

CHRISTMAS MESSAGES.

Here in England, the Jolly old man of Christmas our children refer to as 'Father Christmas'. Like children all over the World they send him letters. Our busy little English Robin would surely love to help. The clearing in the woods is dressed in winters green as in England a white Christmas is sadly very rare.

Background Colours
DecoArt	Buttermilk,
"	Brandy Wine,
"	Asphaltum.

Painting Colours.
DecoArt	White Wash,
"	French Vanilla,
"	Moon Yellow,
"	Yellow Light,
"	Deep Midnight Blue,
"	Lamp Black,
"	Black Green,
"	Teal Green,
"	Asphaltum,
"	Charcoal Grey,
"	Brandy Wine,
"	Cadmium Red,
"	Dioxazine Purple,
"	Neutral Grey,
"	Desert Turquoise,
"	Raw Sienna,
"	Flesh Tone,
"	Burnt Sienna,
"	Delane's Cheek colour,
"	Orchid,
"	Sapphire,
"	Cadmium Orange,
"	Cadmium Yellow,
"	Eggshell,
"	Driftwood,
"	Honey Brown,
JoSonja	Warm White,
"	Titanium White.

Additional Materials.
JoSonja	Flow medium,
"	Retarder/Antiquing medium,
"	Clear Glaze medium,

Masking Fluid (mix of Copydex +water
1 : 3).

Brushes.
18 (3/4") Flat wash,
4 Fan,
3 or 4 Old round for Copydex mix,
4 Round (Natural hair),
2 or 3 Liner,
6 Flat wash,
1/8" Deerfoot,
Old Toothbrush to Fleck surface.

BACKGROUND PREPARATION.
1. Sand Sleigh with 220 grit sandpaper and brush away dust.

2. Basecoat runners, bottom and sides with a mix of **Brandy wine + Clear Glaze Medium 4 :1. Dry,** Gently sand and give a second coat. Now dry.
3. Working these area's one section at a time, moisten with Retarder then Antique with **Asphaltum.** Use your Fan brush to even and soften strokes. Dry. Continue with other basecoated areas.
4. Protecting the unpainted Top, fleck the Red area's with a mix of **Asphaltum + a touch of Black** with water to thin a little. Dry.
5. Give the entire red area a protective coat of Clear Glaze Medium then dry.
6. Basecoat the Top area with a mix of **Buttermilk + Clear Glaze Medium 4 : 1.**
   Lightly sand and give a second coat. Dry.
7. Transfer only enough design to guide you. Omit all the Ivy leaves, transfer these after your background is set in.
8. Dress the old #3 or 4 Round brush with soap to protect it then tint the Copydex mix with a tiny touch of **Yellow Light** (so that you can see it better). Now mask off Moon, Tree trunk and larger branches, Father Christmas and his wife, Robins and the large log. Make sure you don't miss any areas. The masked areas dry quickly.

PAINTING YOUR DESIGN.
Sky.
1. Moisten the sky with Retarder using your large Flat wash brush, then, loading the same brush with **Deep Midnight Blue** and starting at the horizon, wash in the dark sky. As you near the Moon, apply less paint to give a lighter glow. Even and soften strokes with your Fan brush. Dry using only a warm setting on your hair drier.
2. Re-moisten the sky area and darken the outside edges with a brush blend of **Deep Midnight Blue + a touch of Lamp Black**. Again soften with your Fan brush and dry using only warm setting on the Hair drier.

Forest Clearing.
1. Moisten entire area with Retarder. Now with a brush of **Asphaltum + Black Green** (casually mixed), paint the whole area, then using your Fan brush, move the paint in small upward strokes to give a Grass tuft effect. Warm dry.

Background Trees on the horizon.
1. Moisten the Tree areas with Retarder. Now using your Deerfoot brush, stipple **Black Green** to form the two Fir trees on the left and shrub on the right side. Fan brush the branch like shrub. Warm dry.

At this point, peel away mask (if your background is at all moist you will remove your background). If you find it difficult to lift, moisten a cotton bud with water and gently work the masked area.

Trees
1. Linerwork the twiggy branches with **Buttermilk**.
2. Moisten the tree trunk and larger branches then using your round brush paint with thinned **Charcoal Grey** , off loading more colour in the shaded areas. Use your Liner brush to work the twiggy branches. Dry.
3. With a side loaded technique and **Charcoal Grey**, shade where branches cross each other and also darken shaded areas of the tree.
4. Using your round brush, dry brush JoSonja **Warm White** to highlight. Use your Liner brush for the smaller branches.

Log (Father Christmas is sat on it).
1. Moisten entire area with Retarder then, using your Round brush and a blend of **Charcoal Grey** + a touch of **Raw Sienna,** swirl in the cut off section.
2. With your Deerfoot, stipple Bark area of the log with **Charcoal Grey**. Dry.
3. Re-moisten entire area, shade with a brush blend of **Charcoal Grey + Hauser Dark Green**. Dry.
4. Dry brush with JoSonja **Warm White to highlight.**

Father and Mrs Christmas.
Dress
1. Moisten area with Retarder and basecoat with thinned **Honey Brown**. Clear lighter areas with a clean brush moistened with Retarder. Wipe brush and pat blend to soften.
2. Re-moisten with Retarder and shade with a brush blend of **Brandy Wine** + A touch of **Asphaltum**. Dry.
3. Re-moisten with Retarder and Tint here and there with **Desert Turquoise**. Dry.
4. Dry brush with JoSonja **Warm White.**

Dress Front and Apron.
1. If needed, re-basecoat these areas with **Buttermilk** then dry.
2. Working one area at a time, moisten with Retarder then shade with a thinned brush blend of **Deep Midnight Blue** plus a touch of **Asphaltum**. Dry.
3. Re-moisten with Retarder and tint here and there with **Desert Turquoise**. Dry.
4. Dry brush with JoSonja **Warm White.**
   Note: Paint the Lace with thinned **White Wash** After painting neck and cloak.

Cloak interior, Father Christmas's jacket and Hat.
1. Tip your brush in Clear Glaze Medium, now **Brandy Wine** to basecoat these Red areas. Dry. Now repeat this step.

2. Working one area at a time to completion. Moisten with Retarder then shade with a brush blend of **Asphaltum + Dioxazine Purple**. Dry.
3. Dry brush **Cadmium Red** in lighter areas.
4. Dry brush **Cadmium Orange** to lighten more.
5. Dry brush a little JoSonja **Warm White** to catch light areas.
6. Linerwork Button with **Lampblack**. Dry. Highlight with a dry brush of JoSonja **Warm White** .

Cloak exterior
1. Moisten areas with Retarder and basecoat with thinned **Hauser Dark Green** then, using a clean Retarder moist brush, clear lighter areas. Wipe brush and pat blend to soften. Now dry.
2. Re-moisten with Retarder and shade folds with a brush blend of **Deep Midnight Blue + Asphaltum**. Dry.
3. Re-moisten with Retarder and tint here and there with **Desert Turquoise**. Dry.
4. Dry brush highlight areas with JoSonja **Warm White.**

Lining of Father Christmas's Jacket.
1. Solidly paint the lining of Father Christmas's jacket with **Teal Green**. Dry.
2. Shade with a brush blend of **Teal Green + Dioxazine purple.**

Socks.
1. Moisten areas with Retarder. Basecoat with **Hauser Dark Green.**
2. Using a clean Retarder moistened brush, pull out colour to form stripes.
3. On a still slightly moist base, linerwork stocking stitch design with a brush blend of **Hauser Dark Green + Deep Midnight Blue**. Dry.
4. Re-moisten with Retarder and shade with the same brush blend as above.

Trousers and Boots
Working one area at a time:
1. Moisten area with Retarder. Basecoat with **Asphaltum**, working lighter areas with less colour and with more colour in folds and shaded areas. Dry
2. Re-moisten with Retarder and shade with a brush blend of **Asphaltum + Deep Midnight Blue**. Dry.
3. Re-moisten with Retarder and tint here and there with **Brandy Wine**.
   Tint the Boots with touches of **Desert Turquoise**. Dry.
4. Dry brush with JoSonja **Warm White.**
5. With your Liner brush and a brush blend of **Deep Midnight Blue + Asphaltum**, paint the eyelets and laces.

Entire Head areas (under hair), Face and Hands.

1. Tip round brush with Clear Glaze Medium the pick up **Fleshtone**. Basecoat all flesh areas . Dry and repeat.
2. Transfer minimal features and linerwork the lines with thinned **Burnt Sienna**.
3. Moisten face with Retarder and shade with a brush blend of **Burnt Sienna + a touch of Raw Sienna**. Pat blend to soften strokes. On a still moist base, lighten above eyes, top of nose and high cheek areas with **White Wash.** Dry.
4. Linerwork Eyeball with **Sapphire** and the Pupil with **Deep Midnight Blue.** Add white corners to each side of the eyeballs. At this time Linerwork thinned **Burnt Sienna** age lines. Dry.
5. With a small flat brush and **Deep Midnight Blue,** shade the Eyes underneath the Eyelashes. Now lighten the lower left side of the Eyeball with **White Wash** and put a dot of **White Wash** for a sparkle. Dry.
6. Re-moisten lower cheek areas with Retarder and pink with **Delanes Cheek colour.** Dry.
7. Re-moisten the lower cheek area and tint with **Orchid.**
8. Linerwork lips with thinned **Delanes Cheek Colour.** Dry.
9. Shade lips with thinned **Burnt Sienna.** Highlight with a dry brush of JoSonja **Warm White.**
10. Evaluate your shading in the flesh area's and if necessary deepen with a brush blend of **Burnt Sienna + Deep Midnight Blue.** Thin this colour and paint in fingernails. Dry then dry brush them with JoSonja **Warm White.**

Hair, Beard and Moustache.

1. Working one area at a time, moisten with Retarder and brush in **Neutral Grey,** brush heavier in darker areas. Dry.
2. Re-moisten with Retarder and shade with **Neutral Grey** plus a touch of **Lamp Black.**
3. Using various values of **Grey**, linerwork Hair and finally linerwork **White Wash. Dry.**
4. Dry brush JoSonja Titanium **White** to highlight.

Note: Paint Father Christmas's hair first, followed by his Beard and lastly his Moustache.

Fur around cap and sleeves.

1. Moisten all the areas with Retarder then using your Deerfoot and **Neutral Grey,** stipple the fur areas. Dry.
2. Re-moisten with Retarder. Stipple with JoSonja **Warm White**. Dry.
3. Re-moisten with Retarder and shade with **Raw Sienna** and a brush blend of **Asphaltum + Deep Midnight Blue.** Dry.
4. Dry brush JoSonja **Titanium White** to highlight area's.

Mrs Christmas's Cap.

1. Re-transfer inner guidelines faintly. Moisten entire area with Retarder. Brush with thinned **White Wash** for the Cap. Dry.
2. Using your small flat brush, float **White Wash** edges around the ruffled edge. Reinforce the lighter area's with **White Wash.** Dry.

Robins.

Refer to pages 42 - 43 for worksheet and information on the Robins and letters.

Ivy.

1. Transfer your Ivy leaves.
2. Using your Round brush and thinned **Hauser Dark Green**, paint in your Ivy leaves.
3. Moisten leaves with Retarder and shade the larger ones with a brush blend of **Hauser Dark Green + Deep Midnight Blue.**
4. On a still moist base, lighten one side of the leaf with **Yellow Light.**
5. Linerwork stems with **Hauser Dark Green.**
6. Highlight stems and leaf veins with a linerwork of **French Vanilla.** Dry.
7. Dry brush JoSonja **Warm White** to highlight.

Evaluate your shading around Feet, Robins, Log and base of Trees. If you need to, re-moisten area with Retarder and shade with a brush blend of **Asphaltum + Deep Midnight Blue.**

After 24 hours, varnish with a water based Satin varnish and again after a further 24 hours apply paste Wax and buff.

WREATH AND TREE ORNAMENT

Dowel

Cut letters from card and pop in beaks

Dowel to help fit among wreath twigs

Cut all Robins and small Letter box in ¼" Pine

51

FARMYARD CHILDREN AND
FRIENDS. TABLE

**Suggested Designs for side
panels of the Table**